THE AMERICAN DREAM FROM AN INDIAN HEART

THE AMERICAN DREAM FROM AN INDIAN HEART
Living to Learn and Learning to Live

By

Krish Dhanam

FOREWORD

By

Zig Ziglar

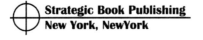

Strategic Book Publishing
New York, NewYork

Strategic Book Publishing
An imprint of AEG Publishing Group
845 Third Avenue, 6th Floor - 6016
New York, NY 10022
www.StrategicBookPublishing.com

ISBN : 978-1-60693-227-8   1-60693-227-6

Printed in the United States of America

Book Design: SP

DEDICATION

This book is dedicated to my bride Anila, and my son Nicolas, who have completed every facet of my life, and whose walk with me in spirit and faith have strengthened me as a husband and father.

TABLE OF CONTENTS

Foreword..11

Acknowledgements..13

Introduction...15

Chapter 1   Pride, Poverty, and Possibility...................19

Chapter 2   Faith and Freedom....................................41

Chapter 3   Discipline and Dignity..............................59

Chapter 4   Hitch Your Wagon to a Star.......................93

Chapter 5   Forty-Five Hours of Productivity............117

Chapter 6   You Can, Too...143

Chapter 7   The Privilege of Work..............................159

FOREWORD

I am honored to have been asked, and it is with great pleasure and yes, even pride, that I write this foreword for Krish Dhanam's exciting new book, *The American Dream from an Indian Heart.* I am honored because over the 17 years that Krish Dhanam has been working with our company, he has lived a life that bears witness to his love for God, his love for his family, and his impeccable work ethic. It is a pleasure because he has faithfully, loyally, and always to the very best of his ability, served in every capacity we have asked him to. I write this with pride because Krish Dhanam is a real life example of what I have been teaching the past 50 years, "You can have everything in life you want if you will just help enough other people get what they want." I am pleased to be able to recommend that you read and take to heart the words of a man I have come to admire, respect, and love.

It is a fact that legal immigrants are four times more likely to become millionaires than native-born Americans. Krish's observant nature has allowed him to draw insightful conclusions about why this is true. If you are reading this book in India, America, or anywhere else, if you want more of the things money will buy and all of the things money cannot buy, you are reading the right book.

Krish brought to life the dream he embraced as an eight-year-old boy gazing up at the stars on a crowded beach in India. He knew that those same stars shone over America and he determined that one day he would live there. On March 1, 1986, Krish followed his new bride Anila and arrived in New York with $9.00 to his name. I don't want to tell you too much of his story, he does a much better job of that than I can, but I will tell you that today he owns a beautiful home and has a bright, loving son, Nicolas. He serves as Co-founder of Krish Dhanam Training International In., the President of Mala Ministries Inc, and a Consultant to Ziglar Worldwide, and is a much sought after international speaker.

By the time you have finished reading this captivating book you will fully understand how to enjoy the things that truly matter in life and you will have at your disposal practical, easy to apply strategies to achieve your dreams. Read carefully, pray fervently, and get busy. Krish teaches well what his lifetime of living has taught him. Apply what you learn here and I will *See You At The Top*!

Zig Ziglar

ACKNOWLEDGEMENTS

First and foremost, I would like to thank my bride Anila, whose constant sacrifices have allowed me to embark on a career that has seen her endure lengthy absences from me. Her quiet grace and dignity have strengthened me beyond belief. To my son Nicolas, I simply want to say what I have said to you every night for many years-"You are mine and I love you, you are terrific and I am proud of you." Dad and Mom, your inspiration can never be justified with ink and the tears that would do justice will flow for as long as I have breath. Thank you for who you are and who you have allowed me to become.

Mr. Ziglar's role in my life has been well documented and my gratitude for his generosity in time and talent is amplified by his kind words in introducing this book. His example in living a balanced life is the inspiration behind a majority of my journey. "Sir, I can never repay you for what you have given me, but will try to show others your philosophy and wisdom for as long as I live."

There are many others who have played significant roles and I hope I do not leave anyone out. Subbi my brother, your rise to the pinnacle of your profession is proof that "hard work pays." You are the embodiment of determination and your love for me as your little brother overwhelms me.

Laurie Magers, who has played the role of my American mom, garners praise for the ongoing encouragement she has given me every working day. Her guidance in my life has been invaluable since my own parents live half a world away. To Julie Ziglar Norman I owe the outcome of this book. Her insights and superior editing capabilities have made it what it is. Richard Oates a former colleague and close friend, is to be credited for the title of the book and has my immense gratitude for picking me up the many times I was down.

I would be remiss if I did not publicly thank my in-laws, Raj and Maya Michael, who allowed me to take their daughter's hand in marriage and directly lead me to Jesus Christ. Dr. Jim Ozier, my beloved pastor, baptized me along with my son, gave me a new hope, and renewed vision, and for this I have ample reason to be eternally grateful. My spiritual mentor, Dr. Ramesh Richard, has guided my growth and allowed me to learn the value of a servant's heart. "Thank you Ramesh Anna for allowing me to walk beside you as an observer all over the world."

To the many others who have crossed my path and validated my choices, I salute you. A special thanks to my colleague Bryan Flanagan who helped me in many ways. I hope I have done justice to some of the lessons he has taught me. The organizations that used my services and gave me a platform to ply my craft deserve a special thank you. Finally, I would like to thank America for allowing this immigrant to have a chance to dream the American dream.

INTRODUCTION

We all have potential that is limitless when compared to the extent to which we have used our talents. Truly we have not begun to scratch the surface of what we are capable of achieving. Martin Luther King said that God has given us all the power to accomplish great things and that He has given some of us more than others, but He has not left any of us without some talent to build on.

Much has been written about the psychology of achievement and still more about the need to motivate oneself. It has also been believed that in the world today success or failure can be determined by the effort we put out and the results we want. *By contrast, in the remote parts of developing nations most people believe that their position in life is predestined and their condemnation to poverty is a given.* However, in these same dwellings of human discontent lie small dreams and huge hopes. My life began amidst such doubt and uncertainty. *As sure as the sunshine of optimism greets each capitalistic dawn in one place, the dusk of discontent settles over malnourished souls in many other places.* We live in mixed and turbulent times and some meander through life devoid of hope. The world that gave us the beginning of space exploration and the incredible landing on the moon, also gave us the incomprehensible spectacle of ethnic cleansing in the former Yugoslavia. The concepts outlined in this book are opinions amassed in a journey that has taken me from rural parts of Southern India to the United States of America.

The pursuit of happiness in the urban jungle has reduced people to predators of indecency. We have striven for perfection while losing the shine that comes from innocence. With animal like curiosity, we have learned greed and with adolescent impatience, we have mocked morality. As a society, we face bankruptcy in the treasury of humanity. The gurus and pundits of optimism and the peddlers of pessimism all agree on the need for change. Who will orchestrate this symphony, and who will provide the backdrop as an entire generation waits for the world to change?

The opinions and suggestions outlined in this book are meant to give a survivalist instinct to anyone who wants to achieve excitement, success, enthusiasm and a powerful work ethic. The parallels between India and America are drawn because of the personal strength I have received in the comparative advantages of these two very different democracies. The musings of my wandering mind are beliefs I have adopted after being a spectator to human behavior all over the world. When you deal with the tough social issues of welfare, homelessness, and reform in one place, and compare them to the ravaged ruins of a country like Rwanda, perspectives of hope change. At times the suggestions will come across as harsh, and I ask for the forgiveness of the reader. I do hope that this book will inspire you to think individually and restore in yourself the hopes, dreams and ambitions that were an integral part of your own innocence. Periodically references are made to two Indians from my own childhood. One is Meena, a child bride, and the other is Mohan, a rickshaw driver. Their journeys through life and the comparisons drawn between their daily routines and the routines of those more privileged are illustrated so that we all can see how truly blessed we are.

Do not let the color of your skin, the hue of your anger, or the tint of your resentment prevent you from experiencing the greatest journey of all. The privilege you have of riding the bus of liberty across the plains of hope to reach the promise of unchallenged happiness is known to very few in this lifetime of ours. I do believe that success has a color and survival has a shade. Neither of these two events is made of the color you see through your eyes, but the color you feel in your soul. I was born brown and will die brown. In all of my journeys, I will never expect complete understanding of someone who has not had the same exact experience. So if you are different in any way, remember the extent of your success is what you want it to be. **This message is designed to encourage you to take the canvas of hope and the brush of a glorious vision and paint your own portrait of excellence.**

I

Pride, Poverty and Possibility

A man looked at a peanut, caught a vision of a better world, and spent the rest of his life devoted to the possibilities of a peanut*. In another part of the same world, someone was probably looking at a peanut with the sole objective of overcoming hunger by eating it. This scenario has been repeated in almost every walk of life. *Some see poverty and want to escape it any way they can. Others live within it and ponder the possibilities.*

Meena was washing the dishes in the narrow street that ran behind her house. Her home was a sheet of asbestos that covered four walls of tin, insulated with plastic to withstand the elements. The water that dripped from the faucet was in short supply and had the faint odor of rust as it came through the corroded pipes. Using the husk of a coconut as a brush and the rind from used tamarind as soap, she polished the household's two plates. At the age of fourteen, this child bride had pride in her role as a woman.

*As a scientist George Washington Carver's work resulted in the creation

19

of 325 products from peanuts, more than 100 products from sweet potatoes, and hundreds more from a dozen other plants native to the Southern United States. These products contributed to rural economic improvement by offering alternative crops to cotton that were beneficial for the farmers and for the land.

Her dreams washed away with the tide of uncertainty and her hopes were shrouded in the marital vows taken by her parents who paid for her to have this life. This is India- "My India." As I grew up in the belly of her being, I saw people like Meena all around me.

Mohan is a rickshaw driver plying his craft on the streets of Kolkatta. He lives in a slum on the banks of a river overflowing with filth and refuse. Pollution is the air he breathes, decadence is the street he walks on, and shame and despondence are his neighbors. With one step following the next on burning asphalt roads, Mohan transports people for a meager compensation that will not even buy the members of his family one square meal. Yet, Mohan honors his father, respects his mother, loves his wife, and hopes that one day he will be able to get a better life for his two daughters. Meanwhile, oblivious to their circumstances, Mohan's two daughters play outside their small thatched dwelling with a vision that one day they will be married to someone their father can afford. *A dowry is being saved so someone can live with borrowed pride and instilled hope for the rest of her life.* Is this man ignorant in his belief or is his so-called belief so lop-sided that he cannot see beyond it? For Mohan and many others like him, the choice of living with the condition and making the most of circumstance is already made. My good friend John Foppe says, "Sometimes it is better to have the condition than let the condition have you." John Maxwell says the poorest people in the world are not those who do not have "stuff" - the poorest people in the world are those who do not have a vision that tomorrow will be better.

Meena and Mohan have a unique type of pride and, more importantly, the awesome ingredient called self-respect. In a developed country like America or England, it is inconceivable to imagine something so audacious. How can people with nothing to their names have pride in their being? How can people with no destination have the guts and the gall to look at an itinerary for their lives? Is their journey of condemnation not the fault of those who have much? Are they not paying for someone's sins? No. God in his infinite wisdom created this world. He carved man out of his own image.

Genesis 1:27 – So God created people in his own image. God patterned them after himself; male and female he created them.

Yes, this benevolent God created the poor and the rich. *The ability to live and exist is not a birthright. In fact, the ability to survive is not a given assurance. Dealing with the hand you are dealt is not a gamble. In and of itself, poverty has a virtue that when left alone can encompass pride.* On a personal note, my mother was married to my father at the age of fourteen. A sure statistic for marital failure if you listen to those who think they know more than you do. As a child-bride my mother accepted her role and joined the ranks of motherhood by the time she was sixteen. However, she did not become a statistic of teenage pregnancy, nor did she succumb to the welfare rolls. India has no welfare system or social security provision to succumb to. *Think about the simplicity. If you don't have a level to stoop to, you won't. It's not the intelligence of knowing that makes the*

21

difference. It is sometimes the innocence of not knowing that reveals the resilience in the human spirit. Mom survived because of the greatest currency of all - **PRIDE**. Not haughty or arrogant pride but the pride of dignity and self-respect. This pride manifested itself into the motivation needed to survive. My formula for this pride "fueled with hope" is borrowed from my mother.

P ersonal
R ecognition
I nstills in me a
D esire for
E xcellence

PERSONAL

The first step in any process is the determination that the war of survival is personal. Most human feuds are personal. No great triumph or gigantic achievement was ever accomplished without the architects of that victory claiming personal responsibility. *When you start accepting responsibility, all roads that lead to significance will begin at your own doorstep.* Pride is personal, and the more personal you make it the greater the joy that is experienced in eventual victory. Today my mother walks with her head held high. Her educational triumphs, gained amidst the doubts of those who surrounded her, were the foundation for her personal growth. When the experts of India proclaimed that she would be a statistic of culture, she denied them the pleasure of gloating. She did not succumb to the popularity of what was expected of her, but charted a course based on what she expected of herself. In 1971, she made a personal choice to go back to school. Having dropped out of school in the eighth grade because she was betrothed to my father, she decided to renew her educational odyssey almost seventeen years later. Remember that this was India during the toughest times of economic and social liberation. I vividly recall the day in 1979 when she graduated from college with a degree in history and brought home her accomplishment. *Her tears of personal victory were so genuine that renewed hope is born in me every time I think of what she did.*

What would you like to accomplish in this lifetime that will give you personal satisfaction? ***Pause-Record it-Do it Now***

_____

_____

_____

RECOGNITION

Everyone in the world remembers those first report cards and the family joy as those grades were displayed for all to see on the refrigerator door. Today in the hallowed halls of our working world, nobody congratulates us for the wonderful past, or even stops to acknowledge our innocent wins. If Gandhi waited for societal accolades, India would have had to wait much longer for her freedom. If Dr. Martin Luther King, Jr. had waited for people to praise his oratorical brilliance before he became passionate about the cause, the civil rights movement in this country would not have started at the time it did. *All worthwhile causes had at the helm people who recognized their value before societal salutations became popular.* You will feel empty unless you start recognizing the strengths granted to you by your creator and contributions you will make as a result. It is important to recognize that you are the one who has to celebrate your own victories, giving you the choice to draft new plans for subsequent achievements.

Very few people get unadulterated recognition that is pure and sincere. *If you practice personal recognition daily for yourself and those around you, the results give you a feeling of belonging. Personal recognition is a vital ingredient to move from survival to significance. If done right, it begins to build worth in an individual's journey.*

What are some things you have done in your life that deserve your personal recognition?

Pause-Record it-Do it Now
1.
2.
3.
4.

One of the affirmations that gives me an opportunity for personal recognition is **"Mirror, Mirror on the wall. Here I am. What's my call?"**
"Do not wish to be anything but what you are, and try to be that perfectly."
St. Francis De Sales

INSTILLS IN ME

The goal should be to make positive, clean, wholesome input into your life a constant activity. The research, design and development of your success formula should be focused on improving you to the next level of achievement. Remember there is not going to be any noteworthy change in the people around you. The neighbors are not going to notice your new pride and traffic is not going to part as you motivate your way through the congested roads of negativity. Change your morning ritual to include a daily inauguration ceremony that names you the President of your own company. This installation of confidence in yourself will give you the blueprint for combating a world that is conditioned to accept average performance and relative mediocrity. A healthy self-respect instills in me a genuine optimism that in this world you can start from anywhere and be somebody. The stories of success in the world around us are reminders of what instilling untainted optimism can do for the hopes and dreams of many who started as underdogs in the race of life.

A DESIRE FOR

Michael Johnson set a new world record in the 200-meter sprint and won the 400-meter race at the 1996 Olympics in Atlanta. His regalia included specially designed gold shoes by his sponsor Nike, who had bet a lot of money on and placed much faith in their product. Their slogan at that time was *Just Do It.* A group of people believing in an outcome long before a result was posted seemed to show the world that desire for something in life may begin with those who believe in you more than you do in yourself. The rest, as they say, is history. Michael Johnson's desire was what made Atlanta special. *That day his heart and desire gave him the drive he needed to "Just Do It."*

The desire for excellence is a fire that should burn so fiercely that your very presence should radiate warmth to those around you. This warmth should indicate to those in your path that you are going to blaze through, and stopping you is going to be difficult. My desire to go to America was born in 1968. My desire to be an international speaker and trainer was born in October of 1991. In all honesty, I never knew if either of these life choices would ever happen. **The obstacles that existed at those times in my life were no matches for the desire I had.** I knew it would not be easy and the difficulty of the task posed an interesting dilemma. I knew if I blazed through the victory would be sweet. If I came up short, I would still have learned enough to be overqualified for many other duties.

Classify some of your personal desires into: (Do it now)

Needs	**Wants**	**Luxuries**
_____	_____	_____
_____	_____	_____
_____	_____	_____
_____	_____	_____
_____	_____	_____
_____	_____	_____

Remember that necessities for some are luxuries for others. Desire needs to be based on the reality of what you have coupled with the potential to which your talents can lead you. Many people desire things they are not talented enough to gain. Getting passionate about every scheme that sounds too good to be true is different than having a genuine desire to want something more.

EXCELLENCE

Organizations, departments, cost-centers, supervisors, managers and employees all use this word. Excellence has been suggested as a way of life and a standard of performance. Most of the time the standard of excellence is a benchmark given by someone in a position of authority for expected achievement from others. These arbitrary standards will be accomplished by some, tried by others, and ignored by most. The same thing does not motivate everybody and not everyone has a burning desire to excel. In the arena of self-development, demanding excellence from yourself based on the recognition you give yourself for a job well done is an incredible asset. It will set you apart from those who are comfortable just to participate in the race of life.

As a society, we have trampled on the word *excellence* and painted a portrait of mediocrity for those that want to excel. In India, with poverty and degradation all around, our visibly under-funded education system had superior standards. We were forced to learn three languages through the eighth grade and at least two languages through college. The worst a student could do, no matter what his color, gender or geographical position, was to become multilingual. Though education and academia are revered in India, they are not available to all because of society, caste, politics and circumstance. In the so-called more developed facets of free society access to education and opportunity are available to most. Because of such abundance and its easy access to people, knowledge and wisdom are treated like every other commodity offered in excess. In most enterprises at the end of the day two types of people succeed - 1) Knowledgeable individuals who can

27

understand the complex and make it simple and 2) Practical people who succeed by sheer effort and determination. Excellence then can be achieved by a combination of theory and practice.

Write a personal affirmation incorporating all aspects of the PRIDE formula (see page 22). Once you are satisfied with your affirmation, transfer it onto a 3 x 5 index card and carry it with you for three weeks or until you have personalized the affirmation into your self-talk.

_____

_____

_____

_____

_____

_____

Poverty in places like America and Australia is considered wealth in most nations. If a member of a tribe in Ghana was told that poverty existed in America he would immediately ask questions about the availability of food or housing. If you replied that in most cases those needs are met or could be met with some effort, the tribesman from Ghana would probably laugh at you. *The insults to our dignity are not when we stand in line and admit that we need help. It is when someone canvasses for us, because they believe they know our needs better than we do.*

There is a marked difference between needs and wants. Not receiving a gift at Christmas should be considered a blessing if you have your health and a roof over your head. I have seen many villages in this world. I still have relatives that live in a village. I know that it takes more than a village to raise responsibility and rationale. It takes pride and dignity. We are off course talking about a real pride that comes from humility. Mother Teresa had it and Billy Graham has it. Meena the housewife has this pride as she looks across the landscape of refuse that litters the front of her dwelling while looking at the rag pickers who search for scraps of rubbish to sell to the recycler. She knows her thatched dwelling is a step up for the millions for whom the footpath is their home. Looking at what you have gives you real pride. Demanding what someone else has breeds envy and results in false-pride.

There is a distinct difference between false pride and pride that is built on the foundation of humility. False pride has three elements to it:

i. False pride is controlling.

If your pride comes from what you do and your identity is wrapped in your title, then the pride you have forces you to do a little more each day to assuage the feelings of emptiness. This causes you to be driven by a need that cannot be filled. You are always searching for the next break, the next promotion, or the next big score. Ambition is healthy, but ambition driven by false pride is controlling. Remember that in order to put your best foot forward you should aspire for improvement and false pride inhibits your ability to seek change and embrace progress.

ii. False pride forces you to operate out of fear.

Similarly, if the definition of your inner self is manifested out of the pride you have for what you do, then you tend to be consumed by many things you cannot control and this produces fear. This type of fear is driven by insecurity and a constant need to preserve your space and fight for your turf. In addition, who amongst us has not had to occasionally fight the "turf war"?

iii. False pride demands that you forsake humility and take credit for all of your success.

The natural extension of this fear and false pride becomes your need to fight the battles by yourself because you surmise that everyone else is operating out of a selfish need for self-preservation so you should do the same. This is when you blow your trumpet the loudest, asking others to take notice and pay attention to your accomplishments. In a world where genuine praise is in short supply, we have all been victims of this process. It is not uncommon to see politicians brag about their accomplishments while convincing you that replicating their past for your future is as easy as mouthing platitudes. Beware of false pride as it is a detrimental attribute that does incredible damage in the end.

The purpose of the contents of this book is for you to forsake false pride (which in reality is vanity) and embrace real pride in your journey towards your future. My mother is one such example of real pride. She realized that in order to have real pride in her role as a good daughter and faithful wife, she needed to do something for herself. Her actions allowed her to defy her doubters. The result was she overcame the odds, she accomplished her goals, and she survived – and then thrived. For this to happen, you need to understand the difference between riches and wealth. This will enable you to grow and become the person you are capable of becoming.

God does not discriminate against his children anywhere in the world. However, in the book of Matthew we are given the assurance that He will be with us always, even unto the ends of the earth.

This is an incredible promise. The American dream that I embraced came partially because of this Judeo-Christian promise. It was fascinating to look at this culture through the hungry eyes of immigrant-want and realize the forefathers of this fledgling democracy had figured out that life and liberty only matter when the pursuit is for happiness. Contrast that promise of less than two hundred and fifty years ago with the messengers of hope and change of today. Hope and change are admirable qualities and as an inspirational orator, I have used these terms with great applause for over a decade and a half. I still believe that the dream is there for the taking if you look at what is required of you and demand excellence from yourself before you demand assistance from another. The late Fred Smith Sr. gave the best advice when he said that real joy comes from embracing habits of the heart that require to give more than you have and keep less than you need. To this masterpiece, I would like to add the American dream also requires the element of quenching ones spiritual thirst. For it is known that man is tri-dimensional in that he is mental, physical and spiritual. To search for fulfillment with one of these legs missing is to wake up during the dream. To eliminate God because the media and public education and the courts tell you to do so in the name of freedom of religion is a sure recipe for disaster. I do not know if all believers are happy but the bitterest people I have met either tend to be agnostic or atheistic in their thought process. Ultimately, the American dream was designed after one believed in the words "One nation Under God."

Psalm 46:10, "Be still and know that I am God."
Philippians 4:13, "I can do all things through Christ which strengthens me."

REAL POVERTY

The citizenry of this world are too cheap to afford the once available commodity of dignity. We have ransacked the cellars of human pride and looted the morals that form the fabric of a responsible people. Pride and dignity were once the main ingredients for survival. Today they are considered weak links that allow us to cling to a world that once was and force ourselves to be ashamed by the thought, *What is wrong with not having everything?* When will we realize that our yearning should never exceed our earning? This does not mean that ambition is bad. It simply means that restraint based on ability and possibility actually makes you a good steward of the resources with which you have been blessed. According to Fred Smith, Sr., "Humility is not thinking less of yourself but thinking less *often* of yourself."

James 4:6, "But he gives us more grace." That is why scripture says: "God opposes the proud but gives grace to the humble." NIV

"You can have everything in life you want, if you will just help enough other people get what they want." Zig Ziglar

When did the notion of material superiority supplant self-respect and belief in oneself? Obviously, the concept of poverty we are talking about is the relative degree to which some have more and others have less. Why do some have more than others do? *When will we have equality based on the opportunity to live the life God gave us? Has he forsaken his people all over the world and decided that his immortal blessings would be geographical? I think not.* How can Mohan pull his rickshaw with nothing more than determination on his side as his parched lips and protruding ribs glisten in the noonday sweat? The desire to move forward in any race whether it is for bragging rights that come with insecurity of marching rights that come with necessity comes from within. A resilient resolve that needs to be tapped and then molded by grit and determination is a sure bet for this movement to transpire.

Dr. Martin Luther King's memorable speech on the steps of the Lincoln Memorial inspired a race of people to march forward. His condemnation of the activities of the moment and his demands for freedom rang from shore to shore and sea to sea. During this oratorical plea to his people, he claimed the default of America's promise to her people of color. He cited the Constitution and rightly blasphemed the fallacy of the times for ignoring his race. Those were troubled times when people were searching for a right that was civil and an identity that was colorblind. All I know is that in the bank of justice you can only withdraw comparative interest. Many of the visions of our time will be unfair and our currency will have to be one of condition rather than comparison. Hitler, Mussolini, Stalin, Saddam Hussein, and Moamar Ghaddafi are classic examples of 20th century deposits that produced hatred and mayhem as the currencies of confused people. You can only partake and build on what is available while navigating through life, as you discover what else might be available for you. Waiting to find out what you qualify for will make you miss the right to dream.

"All men dream but not equally. Do not pay attention to those that dream in the dusky recess of their home for that is but vanity. Look out for those that dream by day for these people dream with their eyes open." T.E. Lawrence.

Poverty received the biggest curse in the twentieth century when man in his mortal wisdom decided to interpret the differences between riches and wealth. My father studied under a streetlight to graduate from college and today hangs his hat in a beautiful home on the Southeastern Coast of India. Ask him the definition of poor and he will say, *"A man without pride has no dignity and one without dignity has no chance of gaining real respect. This man will find validation for his worth in the tasks he performs and will live a bankrupt existence while searching for rewards that don't exist."* There is much truth in this.

In his best-selling book, *See You at the Top*, Zig Ziglar stated that people all over the world want the same thing. To be happy, healthy, reasonably prosperous, have friends, peace of mind, security, good family relationships, and hope. As I have traveled the continents, I notice a certain amount of validity in that claim. Though these concepts were first outlined in the book in 1974, they still ring true today, giving us confirmation on one count. Man is a selfish and arrogant recipient of love. When he or she receives it, they celebrate their deserving it. When they are slighted for the job or jilted in the relationship, they blame a fickle society for not understanding them. There are no faults out there. The conditions you were born with are going to remain the same. If you were born white, you are going to stay white. If you are born black, you are going to stay black. Responsibility, like morality, is an absolute. Pride and dignity are also absolutes. You either care that a situation is right or wrong or you do not.

The human rationalization that we all deserve better is falsely founded in the belief that we were all born equals and man has somehow fouled up the grand equation. While it is true that man has certainly played a more than significant role in fouling up the equation, God's promise is for our eternity. Man proposes and God disposes is the best way to look at this.

Gandhi, the half-naked fakir who humbled the mighty British monarchy said, "Love is the prerogative of the brave, for the coward is incapable of love." Using that logic, pride is the prerogative of the satisfied, for the one who hungers for false recognition is incapable of having a healthy self-pride.

One of the great books of our time is titled "*The Light and the Glory,*" written by Peter Marshall and David Manuel. The by-line under the title reads "God's plan for America." I do believe with all my heart that God has a plan for America. It could be the only reason America is one of the youngest of all societies and yet has the most potential of all the others put together. It is probably the one reason why people either accept her or deny her-almost like a religion. *America was built with the inherent borrowed graces of everyone searching for a better life and was built with the foundation of God's love.* While Emerson was right in saying, "If you would lift me up you must be on higher ground," I do not think he meant I deserve to be pulled up. I try my best not to succumb to the common desire that I deserve to be helped because I was born with less than someone else was. Others may have a legitimate claim to this assistance, but I do not. I chose America and she was kind enough to allow me in. When I got here, I did struggle to adjust to language, enunciation and pronunciation, but was blessed with an extended family that taught me some of the cultural nuances required to move from survival to stability. As the recipient of discrimination and stereotyping, I had a choice to make. Do I allow myself to be a victim or do I refuse to participate in the moment? Again, wise counsel from those who had treaded the narrow path before me prevailed and the right choices were made. For this, I will always be proud and grateful.

I remember arriving in America like many others with nine dollars lining my pockets and a dream that required substantially more financing. Fortunately, my new bride had some family in America that gave us a few essentials, a little money to start, and a great support to rely on. Unfortunately, for us, my bride was laid off from her job when she came to India to marry me. Fortunately, for us there was unemployment insurance. As I drugged myself with optimism and laced my enthusiasm with hope, I quickly realized that I was not responsible for my heritage but I was indeed accountable for my future. *There were those who criticized my ambition and others who mocked my accent, but none who knew the possibilities I dreamed of in my heart.*

If you are an immigrant like me you have a better chance at self-appreciation if you understand that your accent may be a given and that the dream is yours for the taking. In most of my waking moments, I realize I am poor. I might have a car, a house, and the ability to pack my belongings and my dreams to take a trip. Nevertheless, I am still poor until I realize the greatest wealth is defined not by how much you have, but by what you are. *For eight to ten hours a day, you practice a skill to make a living. However, for the balance of the day you need to muster up the will to make a life. When skill and will come together you will have unleashed on the world for the very first time a twenty-four hour champion.* The further you run from the so-called curse of material need, the quicker you will realize that *your riches are defined by what you see as valuable.* You might be able to buy a self-improvement tape and enhance you self-image, but the color of your skin will never change. Couple this with the knowledge that insecurity + impulse + easy debt = trouble and you begin to understand the reason behind man's insatiable quest for materialistic gratification. Similarly, plastic surgery could make you feel prettier, but if your soul is not happy, no alteration on God's image will make you feel better. The question that needs to be answered is - are you reacting to someone's perception of what you can or cannot be, or are you looking at yourself and saying, "All I want is the opportunity to thrive in freedom"? Teaching my son to feed his soul and not his ego will be difficult for me because he is growing up in a place with all the comparative advantages of abundance. Abundances like running water, air-conditioning, electricity, and clothes are a necessity in one place and a luxury in most of the rest of this planet.

TAKE POSITIVE ACTION

Throughout the annals of time, the perception of the difficulty of an obstacle has been more difficult than the obstacle itself. We all have our personal mountains to climb. However, if you want to grow you must keep these mountains in proper perspective. That is exactly what Sir Edmund Hillary did. Hillary was the first man to climb Mt. Everest. On May 29, 1953, he scaled the highest mountain known to man – 29,000 feet straight up. He was knighted for his efforts. He even made American Express card commercials because of it! However, until we read his book *High Adventure*, we do not understand that Edmund Hillary had to grow into this success. You see, in 1952 he started up Mt. Everest on his first attempt and he failed. A few weeks later a group in England asked him to address its members. As he walked on the stage, he received a thunderous applause. The audience was recognizing an attempt at greatness, but Edmund Hillary saw himself as a failure. He moved away from the microphone and walked to the edge of the platform. He made a fist and pointed at a picture of Mt. Everest. He said in a loud voice, "Mt. Everest, you beat me the first time, but I'll beat you the next time because you've grown all you are going to grow…BUT I AM STILL GROWING!"

The growth of human beings largely depends on their understanding that the extent of their present misery in most cases is defined and set. Future misery is unknown and usually comes when least expected. Yet there are many people in our lives that live every day with *anticipatory grief*. It is impossible to grieve something that has not happened. Even if you know that something bad is about to happen you cannot start grieving until it does happen. Appreciate what you have, understand the reason for your situation, and propel yourself in the right direction. The gifts we receive and the assistance we seek should only be to get to the next level.

Matthew 6:34, *"Therefore do not worry about tomorrow for tomorrow will worry about itself. Each day has enough trouble of its own."*

What do you worry for in anticipation that often cripples you in the present?

_____

_____

_____

Thinking the situation we find ourselves in has only one escape hatch is a no-win proposition. If my father had stood on the steps of the municipal office and demanded restitution from the British government for two hundred years of oppression, I would not be driving a nice car and living my dream. Sometimes the poverty of our present needs to be endured, respected and overcome so that the generations of tomorrow will have a chance at something good. I would like to add that if I suddenly became dreadfully poor, I would use my built up resolve to struggle so my son would have a better life. That is what makes Meena the housewife and Mohan the rickshaw puller different from the people who call themselves poor.

"The measure of a man is not determined by his show of outward strength, or the volume of his voice, or the thunder of his action. It is to be seen in terms of the strength of his inner self, in terms of the nature and depth of his commitments, the sincerity of his purpose, and his willingness to continue 'growing up.'" Grace E. Poulard

II

Faith and Freedom
Imprisoned by the Chains of
Hopelessness

Absolute freedom of a nation cannot be attained when individuals act out their own beliefs as a by-product of that freedom. Until an entire populace comes together to adopt and embrace common ideals for the betterment of their homes, families and communities, we are not free. We are slaves to the hypocrisy of believing in one thing and doing the exact opposite. Politicians seeking to be elected, as well as preachers and pundits of God's gospel, have been affected by this pseudofreedom that allows morality, spirituality, and integrity to be debated on three different planes. The pulpits call for absolutes and the politicians cry for tolerance. One group bases their opinions of freedom on

41

fundamental beliefs, while other groups espouse opinions that are developed from years of pandering to all sides. Independence in thought and action can exist only if one has an unequivocal belief in his freedom and respects it.

"Independence means voluntary restraints and discipline, voluntary acceptance of the rule of law. We cannot have real independence unless the people banish the touch-me-not spirit from their hearts. If it is man's privilege to be independent, it is equally his right to be interdependent. Liberty never meant the license to do anything at will. Individual liberty is allowed to man only to a certain extent. He cannot forget that he is a social being and his individual liberty has to be curtailed at every step. Individual liberty and inter-dependence are both essential for life in society." Mahatma Gandhi

America is the second largest democracy in the world with a population roughly a fourth of the Indian sub-continent. Discovered in 1492, this is one of the youngest civilizations on planet earth. I do not think it is just freedom that people want, though that is what it sounds like when you hear the arguments that are sometimes political and mostly ignorant. I think it is having an opportunity to have faith in that freedom. Most people lack faith in their freedom leading to speculation, innuendo, and the eventual support group that will cater to the warped opinions that follow. From the time of discovery by the Italian sailor from Spain to the modern day romance of politics and corruption, America has slowly spiraled into self-developed ignorance regarding what freedom is. Freedom is not about the right to expression of opinions. It is not a birthright or a geographical happening threatened by infiltrated borders. *Freedom is not the guidance supposedly given under a constitutional amendment or the opportunity to debate an amendment because another amendment gives you the right to do so under the guise of free speech. Freedom was, is, and always will be an ideal.*

Asking the veterans and service personnel who took an oath and swore to protect that ideal to stand and be saluted by me is one of the things that I am honored to do when making a presentation. I remind them their efforts in protecting the ideal of freedom and their sacrifices in preserving this land give legal immigrants like me hope. Lying in a nondescript place in below-average squalor, people like me found a deep-rooted solace that somewhere on this planet was the utopian society that fairy tales are made of. Many of these veterans come up to me and tell me the titles of heroism that they have received in times of turmoil did validate their choice to serve America. However, to be gratefully saluted by someone who traveled from half a world away, based on a dream, was something they never expected.

WHAT IS FAITH IN FREEDOM?

In the little town of Brest, bordering Poland in the Western part of Belarus, lives a woman who is finally free. Living a modest, capitalistic dream amidst the ashes of conflict and the embers of struggle, this lady named Christina has faith in her newfound freedom. She is a daughter of the former Soviet Empire who now owns two Chinese restaurants while trying to mend a quilt of hope over her family. A construction worker in the building of Soviet domination, she is now building the tastes of a people that are struggling with self-realization. Her report to National Public Radio was simple. "I visited my uncle in New York and we ate at Chinese restaurants a lot. They had generous portions and nominal prices. This is what my people could relate to." The economies of scale are similar all over the world. *We want more for less and demand the same from our freedom.*

WHAT IS FREEDOM?

As a youngster growing up in India, I became the proud owner of a ticket to a volleyball match between the Indian and Australian national teams. As the long line towards the entrance to the stadium snaked ever so slowly, the heat of the tropical sun beat mercilessly on our backs. The anticipation of competition and the thrill of seeing athletes perform prevented anyone from complaining. As we made the final turn we could see the entrance. Our enthusiasm was soon quashed as we saw the gates being closed. "We are oversold, go home," they said. Very quickly, the angry patrons who had been refused entry started a riot and the police who did not like riots decided to stop it. Before I knew what freedom was, and before I could muster a word about my rights as a free citizen, I was hit squarely behind my knee with a police baton. Anger and resentment were rising within me when my friends signaled for a rickshaw to take me home.

As you read this, you are probably shocked at the application of the law. You are angry at the incompetence of the authorities for selling more tickets than space allowed. You are livid about my complacency in the eye of what was obvious police brutality. Let me caution you that I was one of the lucky ones that day. Amidst such degradation for human spirit, my life was one of privilege.

That day many people got hurt and did not have friends to help them heal. Many were hurt by the police and were left swollen and bleeding in the heat of a battle with no victors.

Democracy is a gift. Freedom is a gift. It is a blessing. It will only work for you if you honor it. Americans, thank your nation for the privilege. Visit the tomb of the Unknown Soldier and pray for the men and women who died to give you this right. Wake up every morning with a prayer of forgiveness. Seek forgiveness for yourself for taking your country for granted. It is chilling to see Iraqi prisoners of war denouncing the regime they represent while lauding their liberators. It is equally chilling to see Americans complain about the yellow ribbons that spring up on trees and posts in times of peril. The reasoning behind the complaint is usually the feeling of anguish a protester of war feels during times of war. The yellow ribbon is only a symbol and has nothing to do with the ideal of freedom that allows the people who tie the ribbons and those that demand their removal to both have a voice that is free.

Do not complain about the atrocities of someone's actions unless you have a game plan for your own survival. The decay of patriotism is one reason for the erosion of hope. The prisoners of hope are the ones who challenge the notion of freedom while paying lip service to a flag that stands for unity.

DATELINE DALLAS, TEXAS

On a recent Sunday afternoon, I watched a television program that was offering a commentary on the proposed amendment to the constitution banning the desecration of our national flag. The

45

debate was simple and the moderators were searching for answers to the puzzling question- "is the desecration of the symbol of freedom protected by the right to free speech?" One of the guests was a congressman. His views were innocent and his explanation via the following paraphrased story profound.

When I was a POW during the Vietnam War one of the fellow prisoners did something amazing. He found a small bamboo stick and modified it to become a needle. Using pieces of red, white and blue cloth, he sewed a United States flag into the inside of his shirt. Every night the fellows in captivity would salute this flag. One day the Vietnamese discovered this soldier's flag and they proceeded to torture him. He returned to the rest of the prisoners all swollen and bruised. He hurt, he thought, he decided and he acted. He found another bamboo stick and started all over again. This was the only demonstration he could participate in to show his loyalty to the country he served.

In a roundabout way, I can vouch for the congressman's sentiments. Though I was never a prisoner of war, I was prevented from being a participant in hope until I got to America.

RESPECT A BANNER BEFORE YOU SEARCH FOR THE SHROUD OF SELF-RESPECT

The flags of most countries are more than mere symbols of loyalty and patriotism. They are woven reminders of humanity's fight for self-preservation. They are the pictorial reminders of the strength of a nation and the resolve of her people. For some, the American flag-waving over the embassies in foreign lands is a reminder to those people that hope is still alive. For others, the

46

very presence of the same flag evokes a different message. *I left all I knew to follow my desire for an opportunity that a flag represented. It welcomed me in New York, prepared me in Texas, and allowed me to be an emissary of hope everywhere else in the world.* Yet, I am saddened by those who show anger and resentment at man-made banners while allowing themselves to be manipulated by others who want one flag to be replaced by another. We need to have a shroud of self-respect and self-restraint before admiration of a banner or decimation of the same will give us purpose.

What banners in life give you purpose?

_____

_____

_____

BELIEVING IN YOUR PURPOSE

The year was 1961 and an entire world held its collective breath as the great Alan Shepard was rocketed into space and landed in the ocean after sixteen minutes of history. This was the beginning of America's commitment to space exploration. This legendary astronaut went on to become one of only twelve people to ever walk on the moon. He died recently and the same America that once revered him paid homage to another hero of yesterday. Are the heroes of your youth a dying breed? Are the hopes of our generation dying with the memories of those that allowed us to believe in the impossible? The day Neil Armstrong made his immortal walk and talk, the Russians abandoned their focus on the moon. America had won an important war without the firing of a bullet or the drawing of a bayonet. If life were so simple and innocence so pure, the six billion people marching from womb to tomb in our lifetime would have had a different experience. Rick Warren's book *The Purpose Driven Life* points out some of the simple practicality we have missed in this journey. We have cluttered wants, need and human rationale in one big cauldron and hoped that everything will return to normal if we just ignore it long enough.

For Meena clean water is to some degree based on her senses that will detect the amount of rust in the pipes today. For Mohan proper footwear to protect him from the burning asphalt is a luxury. The pieces of discarded tires tied to his feet with rubber bands is now the envy of another rickshaw puller who has not made it to the city dump today to search for his footwear. For my grandparents electricity was optional. You had the option of having it if you had the money to pay the bill. Asking yourself the questions about your own needs and wants will put you one step closer to gratitude, which is the building block of a hope- filled future.

What are you grateful for as you read this book?

_____

_____

_____

HOW FREE ARE WE?

Are we free to not show up for work? Do we have the right to lament in self-pity while demanding the world pay attention? Should employers tolerate the employee's freedom to take a sick day off without really being sick? The garbled and inane concept that this world owes you something is one of the most absurd and convoluted concepts that man has ever coined. You are free not to work. You are free to play. You are also free to stand on the sidewalk of life handing directions to those that believe freedom is a responsibility.

One of my favorite stories is of the youngster standing on a dusty road offering help to those that pass by. A middle-aged man stopped and asked for directions to paradise. The youngster pointed to his right and said, "If you go that way it's 23,997 miles. However, if you go back the way you came, it's just three miles." There is so much truth to that. With opportunity all around us we fail to acknowledge the truth.

In the war-ravaged cities of Bosnia, Herzegovina, and Sarajevo, you will find no freedom. There is no hope. There are no children who can be their future. However, there is a small ember of burning faith that the worst is over and the best is yet to come. Yet, amongst the deprivation caused by bombs and bullets, people are now praying for freedom. Freedom from persecution and freedom from anger, freedom from death and disease. Many billions ask for freedom - freedom to eat the whole meal without sharing and freedom to play with the stick today.

I know God is watching us as I pray for forgiveness for my attitude towards my freedom.

Matthew 10:8 "Give as freely as you have received."

Dr. Martin Luther King, Jr. said, "Free at last, free at last, thank God Almighty, we are free at last." Freedom is a gift.

In the bowels of drudgery with no sunshine or scenery, forsaken souls like Meena and Mohan have the greatest freedom of all. Their belief is that their life is part of their karmic destiny, a chain begun many generations ago - a link being held together for one more generation so the next life or the next generation can cease to be the weakest link. As a Christian, I do not share that particular belief system, but marvel at their resolve and wish that people the world over would embrace their freedom with such passion and fervor.

DOES FREEDOM HAVE A COLOR?

Since the beginning of recorded time mankind has suffered, experienced, and fought oppression. From Alexander the Great to Julius Caesar, from Lenin to Hitler, and from Britain's Imperialist occupation to Saddam Hussein's crazy fortitude the war of freedom has always been fought. The conquerors have always justified their victory by playing Robin Hood with the spoils of the vanquished. The fallen and defeated always cried foul because the rules of the game of coexistence had been violated. In the twenty-first century, this great debate between the victors and the vanquished has taken on the dimensions of color, religion, social class and yes, even height and weight. Everywhere you go people complain about the unequal distribution of the spoils. They accuse Robin Hood of being an elitist. They want distribution to be equal. They want more than they have and blame the lack of goods and services on oppression. Some even sue the fast-food companies for the over-the-counter dispersion of obesity-enhancing cuisine.

Entire industries and conglomerates have sprung up like mushrooms with the sole purpose of answering the debate and being fair. Restitution is being paid in some form or the other to those who have been oppressed. *While this may seem like the right thing to do, it creates an even bigger illusion for those who believe that if they cry foul enough, the world will stop and grant settlement.* The magic of freedom is just that, an illusion. *While the rewards will not come during the lifetime of those that shout, the ones who benefit from the struggle do not even pause to pay homage to those that fought the fight.* In 1948, Mahatma Gandhi was shot on his way to evening prayer by a man who believed that too much was given away after freedom. The price he paid for giving away too much is now clouded in the economic advantages India enjoys as the biggest recipient of outsourcing. People want her resilience, her excitement, her enthusiasm and her work ethic. She has triumphantly moved from being the crown jewel of the British Raj, to wearing the technology crown of a new world.

WE ARE NOT FREE

I remember the day as if it were yesterday. The dream began when I was eight, and manifested into an overnight obsession. Lying on a crowded beach in a nondescript Southern Indian town, I sometimes gazed at the twinkling stars and wished for the day that I would be free at last. Not free from oppression, or from bondage, but free from habit that had made me a spectator to a life that had run without a compass.

The first day I watched the news in America I knew I was going to make it. Everybody complained of the difficulty of survival. I sat dumbfounded at the thought that maybe I had made a mistake.

Human behavior is strange, because the moment we identify our mistakes, the textbook in our mind opens up to the chapter marked excuse. I remember turning to my bride, who had given me the

opportunity to come to America, and saying, "Sweetheart, we are going to be okay. These people think they have problems."

The crowning moment of this thought process came in San Francisco, California, where I had the privilege of addressing the Immigration and Naturalization Service of the United States. Amidst the turmoil gripping the country in the aftermath of 9-11, I used my platform to convince those men and women in attendance that they had done many things right. I wanted them to see gratitude from someone who had crossed the border with dignity and legality and was truly humbled by the privilege that was given to me to live in this awesome country. The reminder of that day was a commemorative Statue of Liberty made especially for the Commissioner to hand out as a gift. When he presented the statue to me, the blessed tears of hope streaked down my face as the crowd stood and clapped as if to say that they knew all along that having me here was good for America. The first thing I will show you if you ever visit our home is that visible reminder of a journey that has seen hope, humor and heartache, but remains focused on tomorrow.

DATELINE, PANORA, IOWA, JULY 24, 1998

I walked into a room to make a speech and within three minutes of my presentation, I observed the raw emotions of a distinguished lady sitting in the front row. She reached for her tissue and wiped away the tears of recognition as I recanted my immigrant fortune. I was so overcome by her instant reaction that I made it a point to meet her. She revealed a story of huge dimensions and shared a heart laden with the joy that is America. Born in Manchugo (Now Northeast China) by the Siberian border to Japanese parents, Michie had to return to Japan in 1946 after World War II. She met and fell in love with an American soldier and came to the USA in the fall of 1955. Today Michie is living a different dream. The irony of our encounter was made even more special that evening when she reminded me of the importance of my message the next day. She said she would pray for God to give me the words that would impact the entire audience and sell them on the hope that needs to come alive through dreaming with purpose. The following morning she reminded me that she had prayed for me and had a feeling that I would do well. The response from the crowd was incredible and we smiled at each other knowing what we had done.

One of the other participants asked me what it was like for two dreamers to meet and exchange stories of their respective pasts. I replied that it was like two super bowl quarterbacks from different eras talking about their individual realization of a championship. Thank you, Michie, for reminding me of what we have gained.

If you looked at the rest of the world and then looked at your own life, what would stand out as the reminder that you have gained more just because you dared to dream? **Write it down now**

_____

_____

_____

Sometimes we take our freedom for granted and the arrogance towards this all-important right forces us to behave irrationally. Man is arrogant and yes, even conceited about the promise of his own power. With reckless abandon this most gifted of all God's creatures can make a message travel around the world in two seconds, and then not have the desire to make today a better place by focusing on the freedom of the moment.

REBUILDING CHARACTER

The following is excerpted with permission from Imprimis, a monthly journal of Hillsdale College. Subscription is free upon request from Hillsdale College, 33 East College Street, Hillsdale, Michigan 49242. The excerpted text is taken from a speech given by Congressman J.C. Watts, (R), Oklahoma.

Thomas Jefferson once confessed, "Indeed, I tremble for my country when I reflect that God is just." He was concerned about the character of citizens in the early republic – how much more would he be concerned today? I shudder to think what Jefferson would say about Americans in the 1990s. Many of us appear to believe that we can have a strong nation without worrying about our character or the character of our leaders. This is like saying we can swim in the ocean without worrying about getting wet. Character - that is, doing what is right when nobody is looking-is essential.

I sit [at the time of the speech] on the National Security Committee in the U.S. House of Representatives, and I hear much debate about what makes for a strong nation. How many tanks, bombers, and missiles should we buy? How should we react to regional conflicts around the globe that may affect our national interest? Who are our enemies? Who are our allies? How should we deal with them? As important as these questions are, none is as important as this: How do we defend ourselves from our worst enemy, which is us? How do we overcome our fallen nature and choose virtue over vice, right over wrong?

I will take character over bombers and missiles any day of the week. That is because character is the best weapon of defense. However, we have a long way to go when it comes to developing character in this cynical, self-indulgent age. Just look at the moral weakness we tolerate. We allow a basketball player with an $8 million contract to choke his coach, issue a death threat, leave the room and come back 20 minutes later as if nothing had happened. Worse yet, we portray him as the victim! (Both the originator of this commentary and the basketball player in question are black. The coach was white, in case you were struggling for a stereotype.) He cannot possibly be held responsible for his destructive impulses, so our reasoning goes.

When I read this speech, I realized that character in this world is no longer viewed as an important and vital ingredient for survival. It is considered mere nomenclature designed to make people who detest absolutes cringe about the injustice of infringements on the rights and behaviors of individuals.

A couple of years ago the wise and the articulate said that if the budget was balanced and the economy was doing well we needed to move on and forgive the president of that time for an impeachable offense. Those words of the past have since come full circle to haunt another presidency. Corporate mistrust and wanton lust for capital gains that built humongous empires for the very greedy and the very dishonest were built at the time when the economy was doing well. One chief executive of a nation said personal character did not matter as long as the economy was doing well. Other chief executives took that to heart and proceeded to pillage and plunder the very people who made them look good. This time the recovery will be harder because we have lost a priceless ingredient: trust.

MY FREEDOM HAS NO STIPULATIONS

The popular belief is that our freedom guarantees us the right to stray, bray and be gray, but it also allows us the right to betray without disapproval. In the political halls of decayed societies, the crooked politician and the character-flawed statesmen are looked upon with disgust and envy. The generational influencers of this world have unleashed a list of wants and hopes so long that people living in relative drudgery have given up hope. Then they look at the acceptance and relative grade the so-called "haves" have given our freedom and are appalled.

The stipulations of what is good and decent should surpass the need for covert relationships and clandestine morals. We are all sinners and will fall short of the glory of God, but at least we must admit our weaknesses. I am proud to be weak for I can search for strength.

CONVOLUTED PATRIOTISM

The best picture a couple of years ago was the Steven Spielberg classic - Saving Private Ryan. The invasion of Europe and the marching orders for the D-Day landing in Normandy are celebrated incidents of the war that stopped Hitler's evil. Most of the children of that era became the fathers of the children whose names were etched into a black wall in Washington, DC. The nation that earned hatred from its people during Vietnam is now praising the efforts of those that fought for this freedom. *You are either proud of your country or you are not.* You cannot barter your freedom for rights just because it inconveniences you. The same scenario repeated itself in the war with Iraq. Some agreed, others opposed, but all went to bed knowing that they would awaken to another capitalistic dawn of moaning and groaning.

In this day and time, war seems a necessary evil. I do not advocate it but condone its necessity to preserve freedom. I cringe when I hear the rumblings of defending free speech. I shudder when I hear the questioning of authority, and the doubting of the declarations and what they stand for. One day I might be forced to reconsider my opinions, but those I have today are based on common sense, not on any doctrine of biased living. I respect my freedom and hope that I will be respected in return. If someone sees me as inferior and unworthy of their respect, I am free to ignore them and move on. Sometimes it is wise to slow down before you speed up. This gives you ample opportunity to look at the course ahead and decide on where you will require additional resources to overcome unforeseen obstacles.

In the nation of Ethiopia, the people cannot stand erect to salute the flag of dictatorship because their ribs are stretched against their parched skin, forcing them to stoop as they walk. In India, the brutality of the police and the corruption of the officials and the silence of the media made a college graduate like me a candidate for unemployment. The children in the new Indonesia, who pick up the pieces of their future from the charred remains of a burnt revolution, have very little hope for tomorrow. The drought in Rwanda and the practice of infanticide in China cast chilled breaths of despondence on God's people. The new generation in America has so little to offer that we call them "Generation X." A nomenclature gained by their choice in music, disgust for authority, rebellion against decency, and appearance and language that would openly mock the founders of America. However, as I pen these lines and envision the future, I know that if I were asked I would go to war and fight for the liberties American stands for.

One of my friends has said to me many times, "I would rather be a downtrodden member of a free community than a king without hope." John Maxwell says, "If there is hope in the future, there is power in the present." Let us take this power, amplify the surge of human ingenuity, propel it with enthusiasm, and we will have an unstoppable force that will free us from what Zig Ziglar calls, "stinkin-thinkin."

"The life each of us lives is the life within the limits of our own thinking. To have life more abundant, we must think in the limitless terms of abundance." Thomas Drier

III

Discipline and Dignity
Living to Learn and Learning to Live

"Life is the acceptance of responsibilities or their evasion; it is a business of meeting obligations or avoiding them. To every man the choice is continually being offered, and by the manner of his choosing, you may fairly measure him."—*Ben Ames Williams*

On March 22, 1986, a commodities and options firm in Dallas, Texas, hired me. My theoretical accomplishments and textbook knowledge were stocked onto a shelf and my dignity was asked to take a vacation as I began my American odyssey. The first question posed by a compassionate supervisor who promoted prosperity and demoted ignorance was, "You can work forty hours a week, can't you?" Stunned by the suddenness of the query and wanting to make a positive first impression, in a distinct accent I replied with a question. "Can I work seventy hours a week?" His politically incorrect response was, "You are not Communist, are you?" "No, Methodist," was my reply to bring levity to the situation. His next sentence was not very fluent, as perfect advice dispensation goes.

"Dhanam, you are naïve enough not to be ignorant. I think you will go far."

I can well imagine the hue and cry today if someone in a supervisory role verbally informed a new hire that he was naïve, but as a consolation confirmed that ignorance was strongly absent. There would be four agencies willing to bring a lawsuit to the front while forcing the capitalist dream-busters to their knees. Two support groups would form to hold the hands of the demeaned. Governments would ask for an end to this madness, and media would inform a scared populace of the need for intervention to promote dignity in an insensitive workplace. *I do not know what the protocol is but I am glad that I live with the innocence of belief in the future. As an individual who has built on the opportunities to learn simply to have a shot at a dream, I am glad no one heard the verbal exchange that day. I am thankful to God that he let me figure out the meaning of discipline and understand the actions required to salvage my own dignity.*

"Discipline is not on your back, needling you with imperatives. It is at your side, encouraging you with incentives." Sybil Stanton, *The Twenty-Five Hour Woman.*

There needs to be a higher purpose in all we do and success usually follows. Being selfish about the justification of the moment sometimes blinds the mind's eye from all the possibilities that lie ahead.

History has repeatedly shown us examples of individuals who took the bitter advice of the reality of the moment and transformed it into the recipe for timeless bounties.

DIGNITY COMES WITH PURPOSE.

John Marks Templeton says, "You cannot experience anything in life positive or negative unless you accept it. You cannot accept anything unless you make up your mind to do so." The message in that statement is not reflective of tolerance, but one that accepts life as having its good and bad. If you learn to understand that the bad is a prelude to the good, one can escape forever from the best-selling life story - "Victim."

Does it hurt when accents are imitated? Yes, the pain is so great at times, that some are afraid to speak in public for fear of ridicule. How then does one overcome this impassable barrier that many never cross as long as they live? The following from my father offers hope: *"Son, always have a standard of achievement higher than society's expectation of you. If you ever come up short, you will have still exceeded their expectation of you."* This simple advice has allowed me to overcome the seeming strife of the moment and make a handsome living as a professional speaker. For the past dozen years, I have had the opportunity to travel around the world sharing the tenets of hope, humor, humility and happiness. (*Ironically, I am reviewing this text on a flight to*

Athens, Greece, where philosophy and oratorical brilliance are deemed to have originated.) The success of overcoming obstacles lies in the refusal to lower our untainted optimism to enter a debate with those who choose to be ignorant.

My African-American friend Michael McGowan who works with me says that he, too, would have become a statistic of racial debate if his late mother, Mattie McGowan, had not instilled in him dignity of purpose. Michael started with us in the warehouse and quickly moved into a position of training consultant. Today he offers training advice and solutions to many of corporate America's brightest. In the warehouse where he started, it was hot and the work was hard. He could have cried foul about the injustice of it all. Instead, he chose to learn and listen to the advice of those that wanted him to succeed. It did not come easy, but it did come. It took time to happen, but it did happen. The reward came when he was inducted into the "Top Performers Club" in his first full year in sales. Another example of resilience was demonstrated by Michael when in his first week with the company he approached Mr. Ziglar and offered to detail Mr. Ziglar's car. This shows a different kind of work ethic. He was willing to do whatever it took. He realized early on that work is something you do and when done with pride and honor can be a pre-cursor to amazing things. Congratulations, Michael for setting an example of initiative and performance in a world determined to prove that you should not have made it.

If life had a book on ironies, I would be a star. In 1986, I was informed of what I needed to do to survive. In 1989, I learned what I should do to become stable. In 1991, I was informed of a procedure that would enable me to become what I could be. In

2002, I was told to write about what I had done. In 2004, I was asked to publish my journey in the very land that prepared me and sent me on an odyssey almost eighteen years earlier. As I look back over the journey, I am convinced beyond reasonable doubt that discipline was one of the prime factors in the personal growth that has come my way.

What are some unique ironies in your life situations that seemed destined for failure that actually emerged as successes? **Pause – Record it.**

_____

_____

_____

PEOPLE ARE WATCHING

A couple of years ago I found myself standing outside a hotel waiting for the shuttle that would take me to the airport. It had been a successful trip and the training that was delivered to a company we had been working with was indeed very well received. In my reflection on that moment for the opportunities that exist in America, you can say I was riding higher than a kite.

The shuttle driver was running late and I decided to take action, pick up my own bags and place them in the shuttle bus that was standing in front of the hotel. My thought process was fairly simple. If I put the bags in we would save that amount of time when the driver arrived and we could be on our way.

My ethnic looks coupled with the traveling gear I was loading in the shuttle bus led to some mistaken assumptions by my fellow travelers. You can say that they mistook me for a baggage handler who could not speak English, as was evidenced by their respective actions. The first random act of ignorance was committed by the woman standing next to me as she beckoned me to repeat the process she had observed me undertake. Simply put, she used non-verbal commands to ask me to place her luggage in the shuttle. I obliged and returned to my rightful spot and continued the wait.

The next act of ethnic profiling was committed by a gentleman who suggested I do the same with his luggage. Once again I obliged. This time however, I needed to make a statement of my own. Instead of reacting, I remembered Zig Ziglar telling me once that in life you need to respond because people are always watching.

As a training ambassador for Ziglar Training Systems, I have an obligation to represent my company with the highest standards of which I am capable. Yelling at those people that day would have satisfied me more than anything I can imagine. I am an educated, hardworking, honest, taxpaying citizen, and these people assumed I was a baggage handler – many of whom I must tell you are also educated, hard working, honest, citizens just like myself. That was somewhat presumptuous, if I say so myself…and most folks would have reacted but I chose to respond. Therefore, with a smile I extended my open hand to each of them and netted nearly four dollars - what a country!

The reason for relating something that was painful when it happened is twofold. First, it was the better thing to do of all possible options available to me at that time. Second, it was what the man said to me when I boarded the shuttle and he realized that he had made a mistake. He simply said, "I wish all my employees had your disposition." I am grateful that a cooler head prevailed that day, and in my heart I know that I emerged a greater victor than the two people who got caught up in perceptions and mistaken assumptions.

LIFE IS LIKE BASEBALL

On January 26, 1989, I heard Zig Ziglar speak for the first time. I had won a sales contest and was asked to attend his seminar. With slight nervousness at the prospect of learning something new, I accepted the opportunity to change my life. I am convinced that if I had received a monetary reward for the sales contest, today I would be another performing statistic in life. That day Zig changed my life when he sold me on a concept that I interpreted as baseball advice. In life, not every attempt will be a hit, and not every hit will be a home run, but every home run has to be an attempt and a hit. *Advice that correlates to a notion that you cannot always skill yourself out of the dumps. Sometimes you have to will yourself out of the slumps of life.*

Obviously, if you live where baseball is not the predominant sport you need to identify how this analogy will work for you. In India, it might be equated to the bowler who bowls on a pitch that is giving him no support. He can lose heart, succumb to the feeling of inadequacy, and forget the preparation that brought him to the national stage. This momentary lapse could then prove costly. Being denied victory because you were not able to give your best still leaves you with dignity. Losing because you gave up means you chose to let down everyone who trusted your ability. Sitting in a hotel room in Bangalore, I was watching the commentary regarding the meltdown of the Pakistani cricket team in the rubber match with India, which India won by an inning and some runs. To the reader who does not understand the game of cricket it is beating the other team soundly. Like a golfer winning the match on a par three with a hole in one when all he needed for a victory was a two-putt. You get the general idea. The commentators narrated how the Indian bowlers were able to move the ball and create problems for the Pakistanis. The Pakistani bowler who was accused of not giving it his all and letting his team down complained about how the authorities in Pakistan needed to be the ones blamed. They had provided such a lifeless pitch, inhibiting his ability to bowl better. Same pitch, different result. Living with purpose requires demonstrative dignity.

BUILDING YOUR FOUNDATION ON TRADITION

One of the ancient customs still practiced in India is called "Gurudakshina." This is a societal accolade offered by a student to his or her teacher for the education, knowledge and wisdom this teacher imparted. The homage and thanks is one of immense gratitude, given when the teacher says the student is ready. The sign of humility across religious and socio-economic boundaries is simply to touch the feet of the teacher and solicit his or her best wishes. This practice knows no gender or religion. It is the simplest and purest form of respect. Its acceptance is so universal that it has spread to many parts of traditional Indian society. Touching the feet of older people as a sign of respect and source of knowledge is now commonplace. The feet I most frequently touch are those of my parents and in-laws, because of their proximity to who I am and have become. I credit their roles in my life as a part of the tradition of who I am as an Indian. Many of my American friends cringe when I share these rituals with them. They are amazed that an educated person would not want to stop these rituals in the name of progress. I remind them that I do not practice the ritual out of subservience. I do so out of the tradition of respect that I cherish as part of my roots.

There is a difference between respect and subservience. I seek to honor my parents for the role they have played in providing me the tools to master a campaign against life. This gives me dignity. I seek to honor my in-laws for the trust they placed in me when they allowed me to say, "I do" to their daughter. This brings personal discipline and accountability to the forefront. I revere them as highly as I possibly can within the frame of mortal reasoning. I see people around me shocked at this display when in the reception area of an international airport I will bow down and touch my parents' feet. This takes place every time, regardless of whether we are in India or America or anywhere else life might take us.

I can imagine the confusion people feel when they read this, *because it is easier to sacrifice tradition in the name of progress than preserve the dignity of what you believe.* Like the story of the prodigal son, the father always wants the best for his children. *Most human beings will never know the joy of the moment when the father embraces his stooped child and says, "God bless you, I love you and I am so proud of you." Moms have always given us dignity in what we do or say. However, the shudder of the aging father in the strapping arms of his growing boy is a sight and sense that can know no parallel on earth. Believing in tradition has its reasons, and partaking in the respect demanded of tradition has its reward.*

On a personal note, I promised my bride when we wed that I would be a traditional son-in-law to her parents. Because of our choice to live in another corner of the world for our own gain, I tried to honor her parents for the trust they placed in me when they agreed to give me their daughter's hand in marriage. We were in love but my bride was very clear that marrying me and going against her parents was not a possibility. She added that if things were to go right, I was to seek her hand in marriage the traditional way. I made a vow to her parents that I would always respect, love, honor and cherish their daughter and would try to be worthy of their trust all my life. I do not know if I will ever get there because so many things happen in life, but here is a letter from my father-in-law validating my personal choice of the dignity of tradition.

6th May 2001
Dear Krish who is more than a son:

It is a strange feeling when you raise a daughter for 20 years with all love and attention and she comes home from college one evening with a boy by her side and introduces him as a classmate. I was used to seeing several friends of hers--which included you, Krish.

However, the sky came down on me when she told me a few days before she was going to migrate to the USA for good that she intends to marry that special young man –You, Krish. As a father you suffer from mixed emotions –has she made the right choice or not. It took me time to see you as a son-in-law. To appreciate your good qualities and not see you as a person who is going to take my daughter away from me.

Two years of waiting by both of you when Anila was in the U.S. made me sure that you had made the right choice. Your waiting for

Anila for two years proved that you loved her and would care for her. Whatever little time we spent together. Krish, I could see a kind and genuine person in you. A person who had affection and could show it at the right time. Someone who had integrity and proved it. One who was capable of loving my daughter through sickness and health, sorrow and happiness, and through all kinds of trials and tribulations. You are a wonderful father to our grandson Nicolas – a loving and a caring husband to our daughter Anila – a wonderful son-in-law to both of us. We enjoy every minute that we spend in your company. Your sense of humor, your love and affection and little things you do for us shows that we have a wonderful son-in-law and I could not have asked for anything better than you, Krish.

May God bless you and keep you under His wings all the time as you grow spiritually strong each day in your faith. May God give you good health as you shoulder the family responsibilities and take care of Anila and Nic. We thank God for His many blessings that He has given to us, specially our children who care for and love us. I want you to know that we love you.
Daddy

Not a single time goes by while reading this letter that I do not shed tears of gratitude for having made the right traditional choices. I wish every son-in-law could receive the same letter from his in-laws. I am sure that more relationships could have been saved and more children would have been spared the agony of choosing between dad and mom when they supposedly fell out of love.

Thought!

1. What are some traditions you would revive to have fulfillment and balance in your life?

Cultural Traditions   Personal Traditions

_____

_____

_____

2. What personal traditions that you practiced with your family do you miss?

_____

_____

_____

RELATIONSHIP PERSEVERANCE

Picture that you have logged many a mile and are weary from a desire to be validated. Imagine that you are constantly tugging at the hem of the robe of judgment, seeking approval for your contributions on a road that has seen your callused feet persevere. Conjure up the perfect definition of success as you look across crowded rooms celebrating family affairs, while looking for that discerning nod of satisfaction for what you have done. All of these are moments that all of us have hoped, longed, and prepared for on the outside while succumbing time and again to the internal voice saying *you might be a tad late*. How many years should one wait for acknowledgement and praise from the people we relate to on a daily basis? How many meetings do you have to go to hoping for the promotion, only to realize that someone from the outside with a flash of brilliance has trumped your years of loyalty? How many

70

earnings plans have to be readjusted before you understand that profitability is a one-way edict, contrary to the celebratory teambuilding exercises, which seem to be rooting for you? Perseverance in the relationships that matter begins after all the imaginary doubt and mythical defeats have ended, and those that counted on you are left standing to cheer you on one more time because they love you.

A quarter of a century after I waltzed into the lives of some unsuspecting people in a Northern Indian town, I found myself standing in their living room sobbing uncontrollably. I was going to be introduced to everyone they knew as a valiant victor in the race of life, and a suitable suitor in the game of matrimony. In-laws gushing over the choice that their beloved daughter had made over two decades ago were now holding back tears of joy as they feebly paraded around like proud peacocks. Over one hundred meetings of professional disappointment and countless conversations between artificially inflated egos seemed the right amount of perseverance that one had to endure for this moment. The love of those that have believed in you never changes when you can come back through all the murk and the mud and applaud them for the role they played in cheering you on. A father-in-law as your master of ceremonies and a mother in-law as the meeting planner, who chose you as the speaker, become the backdrop for your moment in the sun. A bride of over two decades prays for you over the transatlantic line, rooting you on so her parents will be impressed.

The notorious English criminal Charlie Peace said he would crawl across England on his hands and knees even if it were littered with glass to save one soul from the damnation his "last rites" preacher was so professionally talking about. I would endure

71

every one of those long meetings, altered strategies, and broken promises to see the joy on the face of my in-laws. I would gladly accept all the heartache in the world to return to the origins of my journey to thank those that persevered when I thought all was lost. Persevering for those relationships that matter and endurance for the ones that do not may become the balance we need to strive for in the pursuit of joy.

Thought!

Ask yourself what relationships you have let lapse in the pursuit of ambition and the quest for material success. Try to reflect why those people who seemed to garner more of your affection actually matter less in the end. Call those that do matter this week and thank them for being there all the while even when you ran away from them.

_____

_____

_____

PEOPLE WHO SEARCH FOR SOMEONE TO BLAME LOSE THEIR DIGNITY SLOWLY

While watching a recent television program, I was drawn towards one of those viewers quiz questions. While the question was asked about some legal lines and parameters, the content of the answer surprised me. Then the reason for our ongoing societal blunders became evident. It appears that a woman had filed a lawsuit against an abortion clinic that did not perform her abortion. Yes. You read it right. On the day she arrived at the clinic an external threat forced her to abandon her intended act and, as she put it, forced her to have the baby. I am dumbfounded at the reasoning for her lawsuit. She claims the establishment whose assistance she sought for a personal service did not adequately protect her. As a result, she now wants the clinic to help her raise the baby. You do not need to major in human psychology or be a proponent of immortal wisdom to want to just laugh at the motive behind it all. The same fundamental rights that you and I have protect these people.

Surely, in the journey of life we have seen more absurd acts than this. However, the sheer absurdity of this particular situation, and the eagerness to blame everyone for the consequences except the individual who was responsible, is amazing. The debates by the so-called bright people as to this woman's rights give the so-called victims a motive to depend on someone else. As a forty-two year old professional, I do get a lot of flack for my rigid behavior. My debates and arguments have never been solely founded on religious or political guidelines. They have mostly been founded on the commonsense that is no longer a common practice. I am sure that when this lady decided to embark on filing her lawsuit most of the advice she received was to go ahead because she was wronged. That, coupled with the belief that she is owed something for this radical and drastic turn of unplanned events, seems to rationalize her position to herself. I do not judge her ability to be a parent or a citizen, but I am appalled by her right to pursue such frivolity. Matters of grave interest like education, family values, honesty and human morality need a wake-up call. What if I sued everyone for the heartache I am caused when late night comics make fun of my Indian accent? I chose to come here and benefit from the prosperity that comes from a free society. *If I do not reward everyone for my prosperity, I cannot be allowed to demand restitution every time I feel I am wronged.* Do not misunderstand - some complaints and lawsuits have a purpose to protect the citizens of a democracy. However, suing because the coffee is too hot, or an ex-wife did not wear black to a funeral, is not only ridiculous, it is laughable.

During the last few years, have you noticed that the society we live in caters to the absurdity of relativism? The reasoning behind this concept is there can be no absolutes in a free society with free choice, so everything must be relative. My bride has never asked me if I was "relatively faithful" on a trip and my parents do not expect me to be "relatively respectful" because I live in a culture different from where I was born. As the "good book" suggests, some things are right and some things are wrong. My question is usually to ask the purveyors of the relativism debate if they are absolutely sure there can be no absolutes. By then they get the hint that if there can be "no absolutes" then they cannot be absolutely sure about it either. A catch twenty-two when you lose an argument you yourself started.

Gandhi said faith becomes lame when it ventures into matters of reason. My personal confession is a desire for the madness to stop and a return to a society where people were taught God, family and country. One can hope, love and pray for this return with anticipation. In this anticipation is the hope that tomorrow will be better. In that hope is the ability to dream the dreams of promise and opportunity. Speaking to a group of technical people in India, I shared with them that the dream of technological brilliance for the

Indian sub-continent was born five decades earlier. Jawahar Lal Nehru had initiated the process that would result in the Indian Institute of Technology. Today graduates from that august body have been at the helm of advances and discoveries that have changed the way mankind thinks. The result is that the so-called poor, overcrowded maze of poverty called Hindustan now has Silicon Valley East and Cyberabad. The very country that was mocked on late night TV by comics who could not wait to tell jokes about Babu the convenience store clerk now boasts jobs moving from Bangor to Bangalore. Some laughed at the humor of the moment while others dreamed of the opportunity of the future.

LESSONS ON DIGNITY AND DISCIPLINE

The following is *excerpted, from Top Performance by Zig Ziglar, Baker Books 2003*

On June 7 of 1994, I had the rare privilege of meeting one of the most effective top performers of our time. I was entrusted with the task of taking a donation from my employer in Dallas to a little missionary worker in the backward slums of Calcutta. I was asked to meet and greet Mother Teresa and offer the donation as a gesture of goodwill for all that she had accomplished. Little did I know the encounter, which would last about twenty minutes, would give me some incredible leadership principles that were going to last me a lifetime.

In my haste to part with the money and capture a picture with the future saint, I kept egging this icon of patience to come to where I was standing so a memory of our meeting could forever be recorded. It was evident from what transpired that the memory I wanted to create was not of as much significance as the result of the actions of that day. My camera stopped working and any number of efforts to get a picture were thwarted by fate, coincidence or happenstance.

I left India disappointed at the result and blamed myself for having come so close to greatness just to fail to have something to show for posterity. The *saintly leadership* of Mother Teresa taught me some valuable lessons.

She was **consistent** in her quest to save the poor, calling them "distress in disguise." In an audio series called "Thirsting for God," she told of the many times when she faced the impossible just to be rewarded because of her consistency.

She was **loyal** to her cause. Her acceptance speech when receiving the Nobel Peace Prize was simply "I accept this in the name of the poor." These were the people she was called to lead, and amidst the degradation and decadence of human decay, she found the self-reliance to be loyal to her cause.

She believed in **succession planning**. Even though the world knew her name and her deeds, she knew that one day her role as the visionary for the Missionaries of Charity would end. She knew that she needed a successor whose vision could take this humble organization forward. Sister Nirmala was appointed her successor the day Mother Teresa passed on and continuity was established.

The role of top performers is to learn the various attributes that allow people to go from mediocrity to greatness. Great people do not start out to be great. They follow their vision with consistency and loyalty. When I wrote a letter of gratitude to Mother Teresa, she replied with a picture and a personal note to me. She taught me **humility**. This great lady wrote me a letter thanking me for mailing some letters for her that were sent to encourage the sisters representing the Missionaries of Charity in the USA. Along with the picture and letter were the words "Be a little instrument in God's hands, so that He can use you any time, anywhere. We have only to say 'Yes' to Him. The poor need your love and care. Give them your hands to serve, and your heart to love. Moreover, in doing so, you will receive much more. Keep the joy of loving through serving." In doing this, she proved to be a great **encourager.**

I called this segment *Saintly Leadership* because most of us reading this know that she got her skills at a venue more prestigious than Harvard and from a teacher who was called just that -"teacher." I called her a top performer because this Roman Catholic nun who lived and served amidst the poorest of the poor had her home in the only Marxist state in a predominantly Hindu society.   Dominique Lappierre called this infested maze of degradation and filth "The City of Joy." Yet when she died, she was given full state honors and was sent to her resting place on the gun carriage that carried some of the great martyrs of India. *She transcended circumstances and societal assumptions and rose above the plateau of mortal expectations while practicing servant leadership of the very highest order.* While many of us will not be called to live a life of such exemplary servitude, we can conclude that all top performers can practice the principles of *Saintly Leadership.*

Who are some great leaders you can identify with who practice the principles of servant leadership?

Leader	Principle

In their best-selling book *Freedom at Midnight,* authors Collins and Lapierre depict a scene from British India and do justice to the concept of dignity and pride. Paraphrased their text reads as follows: "One man sat in the corner spinning cloth on a wheel, another sat in the corner reading propaganda and a third stood upside down along the wall in a position of yoga. A fourth shamelessly sat on a toilet that had no door and hid no shame and these were the people who were going to liberate India." Today this man who spun his own cloth and shunned the imperialist forces of Britain is remembered for his poise and dignity. You know him as the architect of a peaceful revolution - Mahatma Gandhi.

"You and I do not have to wait for a great cause to make a commitment to personal service. It can start with those nearest to us: our family and friends." Dr. Keshavan Nair

If we pause momentarily and step off the track of political insanity, we will see that all the great stalwarts of our time had this unsinkable pride and demonstrative dignity that made them visually taller than the common man. How else can you explain the off court success of one athlete and the despicable behavior of another? *Dignity is more than the wardrobe your paycheck affords you. It is a standard set by you.* An exam you have to pass because there is no relative grade.

DIGNITY IS MORE THAN COLOR

We live in a world that relies on perception instead of reality. There are many who are more colored than I am that would react to indignity differently. They might even retaliate at the absurdity of the situation or might call into play words that cannot be printed. *I learned a long time ago that success has no color but it does have some shades. Nevertheless, survival has a color. The color of your dignity as it prepares you for combat in a world that does not see you as who you can be, but who you are. Green with envy, blue with shame, yellow with fear, and red with hatred, this so-called politically correct world is actually blind with ignorance.*

In his book *See You at the Top* Zig Ziglar tells the story of a balloon salesman confronted by a young African-American child who posed an interesting question -Would a black balloon fly if released? The response of the salesman was that it was what was inside a balloon that made it fly and it had nothing to do with color. When I first read that story I marveled at the wisdom it represented. The height to which we can soar in the pursuit of our own dreams and ambitions is dependent on what is within us. Our eventual success may not be what we thought it should be or could be versus what others did with the same ability. Our eventual success will be measured by the dignity with which we accepted the roles we were asked to play in the journey of life.

What are the different roles you play in your journey and do you consider yourself successful in them?

1.   2.   3.

4.   5.   6.

CAN YOU ACQUIRE DIGNITY?

Contrary to the opinions of the social engineers of our time, dignity can indeed be acquired. It is more than civility and manners. It is the whole ensemble of an individual being. It is the internal as well as the external self-image. You have to be consistent in this thought process because if you are not you will face conflict in your own emotions.

Harry Browne said, "Everyone will experience the consequences of his own acts. If his acts are right, he'll get good consequences; if they're not, he'll suffer for it." Simply put, if your inner-self is convinced the world owes you an apology or a favor, your external performance is inhibited by this inner voice. The inner barometer that gives you inconsistent readings on your life hampers all work ethic, productivity and performance. As a result, you are in constant turmoil between what you know you should do and what your belief system tells you to do.

The following steps will give you a better understanding of the process of acquiring dignity.

DO NOT BLAME YOUR PAST FOR YOUR PRESENT

Fundamental to all acknowledgement of change is an understanding that you are not a victim. In essence, this is asking many those people who are truly victims - victims of incest, abuse, poverty, and other birth or inflicted defects that hampered you from having a normal childhood. However, in the grand scheme of things, unless you learn to let go of blaming yourself for the past, you are not ready to begin the journey of enjoying the future.

In this entire book, you will not find another statement that might anger more people than this one. Asking people to forget and forgive their past is amongst the most sacrilegious requests that you can make in America today. *The whole platform of advocacy is built on the premise of past pain.* The funniest part of this is that an entire industry has seemingly prospered with the sole purpose of catering to this platform of pain advocacy. If you walked into the nation's capitol today and asked people to "just get over it," you would be branded a right wing conspirator of hate. You would be hung in the media as an uncompassionate and intolerant human being. If you are from Haiti or Honduras, Eritrea or Ethiopia, and have an accent and the stereotype of your people is cabdrivers and convenience store workers, do not worry. Someone famous once got in trouble for perpetuating the stereotype of Indians and convenience stores by suggesting to a group of attendees at a function that Gandhi worked in a gas station in St. Louis. The muted and rather restrained laughter from the audience told me that maybe it does not take a village to raise someone. Maybe it takes getting out of a village that makes the difference. While it is true that many Indians do own motels and many Haitians drive cabs in New York and Miami, the reality is the combined economic impact of this group of people is staggering. These people have made peace with their past and draw on a deep sense of purpose and drive to make a difference in their present so the future they create for their families is secure.

Back to the Future

The India of Rudyard Kipling was a romantic picture for the discerning reader searching for elusive charm and a hidden lure of a mystic land faraway. The halls of learning at Oxford, reserved for nobility, were the utopia that many an Indian dreamed about as they secretly aspired to matches of cricket and croquet amidst elegant attire and catered tea at sunset. My midsummer night's dream manifested this week on the banks of the Thames as I walked along the cobblestoned streets that breathed a future into the academic royalty that shaped centuries and continents. To learn again about the future of people, I was transported into the past of my wants and desires. I was finally at Oxford where my meager mind began to stare at the walls of a historic college trying to comprehend the personalities that graced this august crossroad of humility and power.

The morning dew that glistened in those sparse moments when the clouds decided to take a break looked like jewels of opportunity on the landscape of vision. The carefully accented teachers of religious discourse had a hint of the glory that was England and the reformation that allowed a new world to be discovered alongside man's ambition. Prime ministers who reported for duty amidst the grandeur of a monarchy seemed to be immortalized in canvas alongside the authors of repute who wrote in the same tavern to different future audiences. Oxford is a true glimpse into a past that shaped a future. Where else can one point to an author like C.S Lewis, whose life culminated with apologetic brilliance as an entire movement of adults and children were left inspired to learn more about the gospels through the actions of a lion?

The future that will come when I return to my home in America will bring with it parts of a city of learning that even the evil of Hitler's advances seemed to have spared. An empire that never saw the sun set on it has slowly been reduced to its original majesty, if there can be such a thing. The God of this world and the light of His truth seem to have been set in stone, only to be told again and again to the throngs of tourists who are interested in the fables of yesterday. Eagerly we clicked our cameras to have digital posterity of the many crests and emblems that all pointed to allegiance and sovereignty when more was believed and perhaps less was debated. An innocence of time where medieval survival and human philosophy were fighting each other for the right to be written about. For about a week amidst the backdrop of such architecture, people from all over the world saw the same England and pondered the past that led them to this point from where a new future will undoubtedly arise. Ah! England. Once again, you have given us a glimpse of what could have been. A truth so simple and a thought so innocent that even time could not change. We are never too old to learn. Early in my career of walking alongside Zig Ziglar I saw a man whose appetite for new information was transcended only by his hunger to digest new concepts so he could liberate the imprisoned minds of eager audiences. The privileges we have in the sheer abundance of information waiting to be grasped, is indeed awesome. No matter how modern we think our journey is and no matter how ancient we think some advice is we need to become the catalyst that fuses these eras so we can be productive in our collective output.

Your Action This Week

1. What assumptions have you made about the sources of knowledge?

_____

_____

_____

2. Where in your past will you look for the advice that was given that might help the present? Whom amongst your family and friends can you lean on so that your learning is complete and inclusive of many different things?

_____

_____

_____

SEEK A RELATIONSHIP WITH THOSE THAT RAISED YOU

Every weekend I call my father and mother and tell them I love them. I seek their blessings and their validation for my journey. This gives me pride in what I do and who I am. I am appalled at the trend of twenty-first century living. We as a people have isolated ourselves from those that truly love us and have ended up seeking refuge in the arms of those who give us false prestige. I have heard it said that other people can give you pleasure, but you will not discover true happiness until you learn to do something for someone else. This has never had more meaning than in the family. Do not be in a hurry to move away from the people who love you because their advice is sometimes bottled in the injustice of denying you immediate pleasure and instant gratification. They do it out of love and experience.

DATELINE DALLAS, JANUARY 25, 2004

The planning for the event began almost a year before when my father asked me if he could celebrate his seventieth birthday with me. Plans were made to allow him to have a surprise party with some of his friends of many years and some of my friends who had gotten tired of me bragging on my dad. What do you give to honor a life of sacrifice? How do you reward a journey of struggle? In which human way can you salute the familial accomplishments of a man who began his journey by studying under a streetlight so he could graduate from college and break the cycle of poverty? The following (poem) was written by me and read by me to my father:

Dear Daddy:

A letter like this can begin and end in only one true and fitting way. Thank you! A small resonance of gratitude for the life you have led and the example you have set. Today you have crossed another threshold of living and we celebrate your seventieth birthday by praising God for your incredible journey.

Your humility and generosity have given hope to many that did not have anything, and your discipline and integrity have yielded promise in two boys who are proud to call you "Dad."

Nothing I ever say or do will do justice to the feelings I have about who you are and what you have stood for. The following lines were penned with an overwhelming sense of dignity and pride, while humbled by the feeling that I was truly blessed to bear and carry your name.

Your journey began in the rural part of a desolate place;
You scraped and scratched to enter the race.
There were many moments in your life when you were sad,
I am so blessed though that you are my dad.

Life's twists and turns sometimes were like falling rock,
No promise for tomorrow – hope's window with a lock.
A family that needed you to sacrifice more than you had.
I am so privileged though that you are my dad.

You provided sweat and then gave some more
A foundation, an education, and a new opportunity for four
Many a thing I never understood as a lad.
I am so grateful though that you are my dad.

Today we stand separated by seas and lands,
Culture, tradition, religion and aging hands
But of the many things that will be but a passing fad,
I revere the moment God said you would be my dad

Happy birthday, Daddy! As we look back on your most recent trip to my home, I will cherish the walks we shared and the talks we had. I will remember fondly the memories you have helped me create through your laughter and joy. There is but one prayer left to say and that is asking God to allow me to be the kind of father to your grandson you have been to me.

I love you and will forever wake with joy in my heart for the good fortune I have in the riches I have inherited from being your son.

Love,

Krish.

From his position at a table in the center of that room sprang my seventy-year-old dad. Ignoring tradition, lore, and the steadfastness that an Indian gentleman ought to express in public, my father grabbed me and hugged me and openly sobbed in unison with me.

Who will you call this week to ensure that you are seeking or maintaining a relationship with those that raised you?

_____

_____

_____

FORGIVE THOSE THAT HURT YOU WHILE THANKING THEM FOR THE EXPERIENCE

Of all the advice I have had the privilege of dispensing over the last twelve years, this is the principle even I struggle with the most. The obvious part of this statement is that you do not thank them in person for the pain they have inflicted on you - you do this mentally. Forgiveness without gratitude is like a pen without ink. It is a good idea but worthless. God himself forgave us and then blessed us with grace and mercy for an eternity filled with promise. Hans Selye, the great stress specialist, said gratitude is the most beneficial of all human emotions and anger and resentment the most destructive. Mahatma Gandhi said, "An eye for an eye will leave the whole world blind." You will never attain true dignity of purpose and being unless you learn to start with a clean slate, and this includes forgiving everyone every day. In the crippled and warped walks of liberated life the story of "victim" is told with much sobbing and wiping of tears. If this cleanses you, power

87

yourself by the experience and vow never to be taken advantage of again. Do not invite the mercenary masochists into the fold and give them the pleasure of dominating your guilt. Therapy is good and nourishing for the soul, but true happiness and closure will come from forgiving others, as you would like to be forgiven.

Matthew 18:21-22, "Then Peter came to him and asked, "Lord, how often should I forgive someone who sins against me? Seven times"? "No!" Jesus replied. "Seventy times seven."

DO NOT TAKE A BACKSEAT TO ANYBODY

During my five-year stint selling long distance telephone service as an outside salesperson, rejection was something all of us experienced regularly. Dealing with the issue of being different in an arena that was not always gentle, I spent many a day brooding over the hostility of people. "Why can't they respect my ability and not ask stupid questions about the dot on the forehead of an Indian woman, or why people don't eat a cow I lamented. *One of my colleagues reminded me that if I wanted to be a driver in the race of life, I should not take a backseat to anybody.* This was one of the first business lessons on dignity that I ever learned. Other people can tell you what you can or cannot be, but you are the only one who can fulfill that myth. I had to learn that if I wanted to have the dignity required to move forward and claim my rightful place, then I was going to have to operate out of confidence and stop confusing refusal with rejection. People who say "no" to us do not "know" us well enough to reject us. All they can say is "no" to an offer. This is good news because it gives us an opportunity to go back to the drawing board and prepare again for tomorrow.

When have you confused refusal with rejection?

_____

_____

_____

IDENTIFY YOUR BIGGEST WEAKNESS AND DEVOTE YOUR LIFE TO MAKING IT YOUR STRENGTH

In 1992, I joined Toastmasters International to begin enhancing my skills at becoming a better communicator. Two people were featured in the manual as incredible communicators. One was Zig Ziglar, whom I work for, and the other was a fellow immigrant named Nido Qubein. As a consultant, author, and communicator he has spent many years shaping the thought process of corporate America. In the pursuit of my own dreams, I set a goal to one day share the stage with these two giants of communication. I have been very fortunate as I write this to say I have shared the stage with both of them. Before I chose to become a public speaker, my biggest fear was speaking in public. As an eager student in one of Nido Qubein's lectures, I learned about taking your biggest weaknesses and devoting your life to making those weaknesses into strengths. The dignity you feel when you have conquered a weakness will literally catapult you right over the negative influences that said it could not be done.

What are some of your weaknesses, and what can you do to make them into strengths?

_____

_____

_____

DATELINE YOSU, SOUTH KOREA, NOVEMBER 8TH, 1969

One of my fond memories of childhood is a six-month long trip to South Korea. My father had been sent on assignment to work as a start-up specialist for an oil refinery and Mom and I were asked to join him for part of his stay. It was an exciting time for a lad of seven who had never been on a plane before. The excitement of living in another country and the praise given by the white teachers was the only intoxication my head needed to swell. Thus began a rebellion that included tantrums and fits that positively embarrassed my parents. The behavior reached a crescendo and boiled over one afternoon as my antics resulted in a non-verbal insult directed at my mother. My father caught this momentary display of brash ignorance and decided to role-play a tennis match. The remainder of the afternoon found me playing the part of the ball as my father played flawlessly on his way to victory in the match. Stung by the physicality of the discipline and scarred by the emotional void, I wept. I just remember two things about that day. One was my father reminding me that in life I would violate many things but I would never again humiliate my mother, for she was *"his wife."* The other thing I remember was the day – November 8, 1969. I jokingly tell people that the moment my father's "Board of Education" met with my "Seat of Learning," is the instant I learned the difference between a girl and a lady.

I am not an advocate of physical punishment, but I am a proponent of discipline. In all the years since I have had no doubt that my father loved me and still does. I am even confident when I say that I never feared being disciplined as much as I feared him not being proud of me. *Discipline will allow you to afford the dignity that is expensive in a world filled with cheap imitations.*

Do not succumb to the cries of people who trample hopes and hinder dreams. Wake up and remind yourself that despite the perceived obstacles, the carnival ride of life will go on. Do you want to fear it or be entertained by it and in it? The choice is ultimately yours.

"The difference between greatness and mediocrity is often how an individual views a mistake." Nelson Boswell

IV

Hitch Your Wagon to a Star

"The lure of the distant and the difficult is deceptive. The great opportunity is where you are." *John Burroughs*

Since the beginning of time mankind has struggled with momentum. Few seem to have it and those that almost get it let it slip away at the most crucial time. Achieving excellence, experiencing enthusiasm, and gaining a work ethic requires focus. If you are going to become a survivor and motor into the future with confidence, competence and comfort, you are going to require a momentum that can only come with focus. Countless books have been written on the art of success, and still more definitions given on the methods of getting ahead, but being negative is more accepted than being positive and hence the loss of momentum. If you live in a situation where you see more negative people around you than positive ones, it is time to hitch your wagon to some new stars. For example, while traveling around the world and talking about balanced living and success, I am often asked why I pay tribute to those around me and diminish my own accomplishments without hesitation. The answer is relatively simple. These role models play a vital role in my life by raising the daily standards of expectation for me based on how they want to see us grow in our various relationships. By having role models in all areas of life, we are able to grow in each arena of life with a specific plan of action.

As confusing as this seems, this strategy has worked brilliantly. People in their respective journeys go through three distinct phases. Each phase then teaches them something and educates them on the necessities of the next level. As a natural consequence, individuals are also demotivated at each stage and take their anger and disappointments through each stage.

I NEED YOU

This is the first stage in growth. From the very moment you arrive into this world you are dependent on somebody else. *The warmth you get in the comfort of the womb is the first sign that you need love, care and affection.* We are the most secure in this stage. As we grow through infancy and early childhood, we have boundaries drawn for discipline and expectations set for conduct. It is in this stage of vulnerability that we experience the innocence of childhood. Here we love and resent in the same statement. We hope and despise in the same stride. Nevertheless, it will be okay. We do not care about dating, mating or relating in this dependent stage of our life. Our wants are simple and our needs are few. Our tantrums get us toys, time-outs or a spanking. Nevertheless, tomorrow we will still have the security of the home, the love of our family, and the dreams of being bigger than we are. There is nothing radical about this stage. It is living with simplicity and loving without condition. The innocence of youth needs to be the binder in which we carry the pages of expectation for tomorrow's trials. Why do we abandon the dreams we have and the hopes we need and trade those precious moments for the drive to grow up? *The culture we live in asks us to be adults before the tears of a childhood have had an opportunity to dry on the canvas of experience.*

The picnics with the neighbors and the fights with water balloons all create a sense of security that gives us joy. Unadulterated joy and undiluted fun are the forces that allow us to expand our horizons and thank God for such a wonderful world. We love Dad and Mom, and all they stand for. We do not like the spanking and sometimes detest the orders, but we are happy for the boundaries and the security those boundaries represent. The parents in immigrant homes are usually shown depicting this "I Need You" attitude. If people spent more time in this phase we would not be separating holy unions at a 50% clip.

Identify the time in your life when you were in this stage. Remember the happy moments and try to recreate some of those happy moments for those around you today.

_____

_____

_____

I NEED SPACE

Most of us undergo a transformation at this stage in our lives. Hormonal imbalances coupled with basic ignorance force us to make choices that start us on a road to independence. This is for most people the stage when the future is non-important, the past is perceived a disaster, and the present is an experiment in futility. Our belief system and the belief in peer pressure force us to choose mediocrity just to fit in. It is ironic that in this stage all we want to do is vegetate. We live, breathe incompetence, and search for meaningless solutions to hypothetical problems. Nothing seems finite in this stage. There is a challenge of everything that can be perceived to be authoritative. Arguments and loud voices are as commonplace as rebellion and childish, attention-getting tactics.

Where in the name of common sense and decency have we arrived at the point of total insanity? The recent raping and killing of an eleven-year-old girl by two eight-year-old boys is cause for alarm. The America that debated the moral responsibility of a president should have also been asking questions regarding the tearing of the moral fabric of their country.

This stage liberates man from his mind and boy from his brain. In the pursuit of selfish ideologies, children have decided to forego the future and act out macho fantasies while extinguishing the lives of other children with a promising future. *In our demand for liberty and independence, have we gone too far in lowering the bars of morality while secretly and knowingly increasing access to immorality?* Look at the pornography and the accompanying messages on the Internet and prime time TV. *We have bastardized the message in the name of free speech, and created a generation of people who are being told that their independence, ideology, dress and moral code are those of choice.* We love this independence, but since the coining of the phrase "democracy," we have never been in such a vulnerable state as exists today. Mothers wear skimpier clothes than their teenage daughters and then wonder why their little girls want to dress in such tawdry ways. Our children clamor for a need for space in this vulnerable stage in their lives and what we need to give them is love and not another buddy. We cannot buy their affection with better toys and an attitude of progression when in actuality we are eroding the foundation. Do not let them get away quicker than they should. They have a whole life - time to grow up and encouraging them to be independent before they are ready is nearly always detrimental.

Meena the Indian child bride and Mohan our despondent rickshaw driver are free and vulnerable. They have independence in thought, being and action. As they grasp for support on the rungs of the ladder of survival they take slow, calculated breaths from the lungs of poverty. Their star of hope is a future they cannot comprehend. The pile of rubble that forms the play set for their children is nothing more than a stepping-stone into something unknown. These are the real stories of dependence and independence in modern India or any country that is developing. Children bonded into labor at a young age so their parents can reduce the debt owed from another loan. These children breathe the toxicity of sweatshops while hand rolling cigars for a pittance. In America or other so-called developed countries, all of those acts would be illegal. Yet children of the same age all over the world are being encouraged to act grown up long before they need to.

They parade their desires in the form of coded messages and secret needs and before the parents realize that junior is grown up, it is too late. These beautiful minds are exposed to corruption of innocence and proceed to mock authority by flaunting skin and desire in the face of anyone who will pay attention. Their role models are equally appalling and the messages that form their affirmations are disturbing at best. We as citizens of the world need to wake up and address this issue of pseudoindependence before the tide of uncertainty blankets an immoral society and floods the hopes and dreams of a free people.

Our children are not one hundred percent of the problem, but they are one hundred percent of the future, and we are their hope for the present and the future. How can we educate the youth of this country to exercise foundational beliefs in themselves so they have a chance at this sleeping world? How do we remind them that their quest for independence might be forcing them to hitch their wagons to falling stars? This second stage in human development has claimed the most casualties but has also been the breeding ground for the fertility of tomorrow's brilliance.

What are some fading and or falling stars that you might have hitched your wagon to? What can you do to correct this?

_____

_____

_____

DATELINE EVERYWHERE

The parents of a seventeen-year-old girl are suing the parents of a seventeen-year-old boy for mental anguish caused to their daughter as a result of becoming pregnant. The crux of the lawsuit deals with the negligence displayed by the boy's mother in not taking action in stopping the young couple in spite of knowing of their activities. The result, according to the accusers, was their daughter's pregnancy and subsequent abortion, which caused immense pain to their child. This is the state of moral decay befalling this great country.

As rational human beings clamoring for life, liberty and the pursuit of happiness, let us examine the insanity of this lawsuit and the incredible forces of inept independence in force.

1. The children were consenting to each other's presence. While immoral, the only thing missing here is good judgment on what is right and what is wrong. This judgment can come from the establishment or the so-called "village" required to raise these two, but should have come from the parents.

2. The parents of the girl blaming the parents of the boy. Ridiculous. You cannot expect anyone else to raise, erase or embrace your child. That is not the responsibility of school, the church, your community, the government, or this country. It is your responsibility as a parent to counsel your child. If the child strays as life has shown us, take responsibility and search for answers and forgiveness as a family. Blaming someone else is a pastime that is becoming all too popular. If it were easy it would be called "Eden." It is not-that's why we call it "life."

3. The judge dismissed the boy from the lawsuit but would let the parents' fate be determined in court. This act of

jurisprudence is an interesting extension of our legal system. How much more frivolity will we as taxpayers stand before crying foul? This lawsuit makes as much sense as "Humpty Dumpty" suing the company that built the wall from which he fell off.

This particular case may have more merit than was disclosed to the public. However, what can we do to take control of our society so that blaming and accusing become the last things we do, not the first things we do? For starters we can insist that everyone live his life with both a moral compass and an emotional compass instead of just an emotional compass. Morality requires us to live in independence while surrounded by the laws of stability that ground us all as a decent populace.

Independence is a difficult and lonely place. While growing through this stage, individuals should be cautious to give themselves a chance for survival in what can be a very cruel world. This chance comes from the next phase when we learn to be interdependent.

WE NEED EACH OTHER

The third stage in growth is interdependence. This is the phase in life into which all people arrive with their worst fears confirmed. After having gone from dependence to independence, we now are accosted with the proposition of mingling with those we have estranged. The society that made those rules we hated is now going to become an ally for survival. We are now the people we dreaded. Yes, we have become our moms and dads. Our appetite for growing up is sated with new roles and awesome responsibilities. Those trendy clothes and funky hairstyles are replaced with boring, monotonous wardrobes and an incredibly straightforward look. Our preoccupation with ourselves is supplanted with desires to make a contribution. We care about the world around us. Those starving people in India and Pakistan playing nuclear tag are no longer a world away but a short distance from eliminating our own world. North Korea's leader is taken more seriously, even though his jumpsuit looks just like Claude's down the street. Why do we go through this realization? Why is inter-dependence significant for survival?

Interdependence is when mankind wakes up and realizes that a fourth of our time on earth may be behind us. Fear overcomes all these people as they search for the identity of who they want to become. Making dad and mom proud is now more a mission than an afterthought. Reconciliation of differences, patching up the bitterness caused by juvenile rivalries, and feeling sorry for the squandered opportunities are the emotions of the day. How then do *we hitch our wagon to a star?* How can we take this self-realization that there is hope and fuel it into our running engine? The following steps will assist you on this path of self-discovery.

1. **Record your Gratitude List**

On a sheet of paper write all the things that you are grateful for. Let your imagination soar. Do not inhibit yourself by thinking anything on this list is too small. *Be grateful for air-conditioning, electricity, running water, working telephones, automobiles, shopping malls, mom and dad, law and order, democracy, unemployment insurance, minimum wage, right to vote, freedom of speech, clocks, clothes and hope.* The list will and should be much longer than you thought possible. As you write down each thing that you are thankful for, ask yourself why you are thankful for it. Then write down a statement next to each item explaining why. Look at the illustrated example for assistance with your list.

I AM GRATEFUL FOR	WHY
Electricity	In India there are mandatory power cuts daily
Telephone:	We waited eight years to get a telephone in India
Free Speech:	There are many places where you cannot speak freely
Traffic Lights:	It is amazing what they can accomplish

Leave plenty of room to add to this list as the days go by. This list will help change your attitude about who you are and what you deserve. The more things you are grateful for, the more things you will have to be grateful for.

2. Models of Excellence

Ziglar Training Systems has a training program called Strategies for Success where the participants are encouraged to identify their models of excellence. The activity calls for the participants to identify three people, historical or present-day, who can be classified as role models. Then the participants are asked to state a specific quality they admire in their chosen role models. This guides the participants to adopt a solution-oriented behavior process based on their models of excellence. One of my models of excellence is Mother Teresa. Her greatness lay in her simplicity. Her mission was to clothe the dying and the destitute with dignity. Every time I am in a quandary about what to do, I ask myself "What would Jesus do?" or closer to home, What Mother Teresa would have done?" The result is living as opposed to reactive survival. This approach will give you more self-confidence and strengthen you daily.

Model of Excellence	Quality
Mother Teresa	Consistency
Mr. Dhanam (my father)	Dependability
Dr. Jim Ozier (my pastor)	Compassion

Who are your models of excellence and what are the qualities they exhibited that made you think of them?

Model of Excellence	Quality
_____	_____
_____	_____
_____	_____

3. Become a Fan Club President

One of the most difficult rituals of everyday survival is intense competition. In an increasingly interdependent society this pressure is magnified because of the number of relationships in force where excellence is necessary. Everyone is competing to look better. The best method to deal with this pressure is to become the charter member of a fan club. Select the people in your life who are the most important to you and become their number one fan. 1) Accept responsibility for all that you have come up short in, and 2) Give **them** the glory for all that has been won. In my own personal example I am the President of fan clubs for my bride, my son, my parents, my in-law's, Zig Ziglar, and my best friend - whosoever chooses to be my best friend. This system saves me from the pride that comes from success and protects me from the despair that follows failure. John Maxwell calls this "The Law of the Inner Circle."

4. **Volunteer Your Time**

In life few things make you as happy as the donation of your time. While giving what you have in excess is looked upon as good, giving what you have in short supply is considered great. When you do volunteer your time, do so unconditionally. I was in the early stages of my career very blessed to be a part of an undertaking in a prison close to Dallas. Four to six times a year I would drive almost sixty miles each way to talk to the incarcerated souls of our society. My job was not to condemn them, nor to forgive them; it was to give them self-esteem that comes from communication. We motivated them to become better communicators. The eloquence that these people expressed was nothing short of brilliance. God made us all equal. Some have chosen to stray and are repenting of that choice. The efforts of this voluntary experience were to demonstrate certain skills and showcase examples of real hope. Today I still volunteer to causes much closer to home because of the rigors of an aggressive schedule. Remember that if Anne Sullivan had not volunteered her time the world would not have known Helen Keller.

What are some areas where you can volunteer your time, and what do you possess as a talent or an ability that you can share during this time of volunteering?

_____

_____

_____

5. Discipline Yourself With Affirmations

A couple of years ago I heard a tape on blessings by Bill Glass, founder of Champions for Life. Bill, a former football star in the NFL, has dedicated his life to bringing the gospel of Jesus Christ to the forgotten and the imprisoned members of society – the inmates inhabiting America's penal system. On this tape he talked about having a ritual of affirmations with the ones you love. One such affirmation that I borrowed from him and use with my son is, "You are mine and I love you. You are terrific and I am proud of you." Whether I am in Seoul, Korea, or Seattle, Washington, I always call my boy and tell him the above affirmation. My boy then repeats the same to me and with this little ritual we end each day. The joy I felt when I saw my son use the "affirmation ritual" as the subject matter for a school project about his father is indescribable. Just the other day he was telling his mother the two of them needed personal affirmations as well. Rituals like this, when made into the self-talk in our lives, increases our ability dramatically. *It has been said the eyes are the windows to the soul. The ears then must provide a symphony for the heart. Discipline yourself with affirmations in your personal, family and business lives and you will see remarkable things happen all around you.*

What affirmation will you coin today for the ones you love the most?

_____

_____

_____

Ziglar Training Systems offers a self-talk card that is designed to bring the discipline of affirmations into your life. You can download your own copy by visiting their website at www.ziglartraining.com

6. Have Faith in Your Maker

Faith in the future by a promise of eternity gives you the obedience of fulfilling your earthly responsibilities in a better way. I know that you do not have to wait until you die to receive God's grace. Faith in your maker gives you an awesome power to tackle life's mundane problems. Nowhere has it been written the path will be easy, but it has often been said that the path will never be lonely if you have faith in your maker. *On October 3, 1993, when I accepted Jesus Christ as my personal Savior, the transformation was huge, but even more dramatic was the overwhelming feeling of security. Today I thank God first, last and always. Do not get me wrong - I do not pray for adversity, but when it has come, the companionship of the Omnipresent has been a validating presence.*

John 3:16, "For God so loved the world that he gave his only Son, so that everyone who believes in him will not perish but have

*eternal life. God did not send his Son into the world to condemn it,
but to save it."*

Poverty has forced many people to abandon their independence
and sometimes this is a blessing and other times a curse. Rickshaw
driver Mohan has grown through all phases described here and has
relied on his interdependence skills for survival. In a treacherous
world, filled with mediocre dreams and tranquilized enthusiasm, he
peddles his rickshaw with fervor. His goal is to pick up as many
fares as he can today so he can take his family to the beach or the
fair. He cannot plan for a weekend because his life does not have
one. There is no vacation, three-day celebration, dental plan or
medical plan. He will not barbecue on Memorial Day or take a trip
on Labor Day. Mohan has no star to hitch his wagon to. His
wagon is a rusty, modified grown-up tricycle. This is the vehicle of
his dreams and the conveyor belt of his ambitions. The money he
earns by shuttling people across the heated pavements of modern
Kolkatta is the income of his present and any left-over money is
the security of tomorrow's meal. His wife and daughters have
hitched their wagon to his pride and will tighten their grasp on his
dignity as he labors each day to buy them the dawn of a life they
may never see. I wish I could tell Mohan and Meena about having
faith in the real Maker instead of just in their karmic destiny.

Yet as we compare the parallels of this privilege we call life,
more people are cursed in their freedom than are in the countries
where bondage is a prerequisite for survival. In 1990 I hitched my
wagon to the star you know as America's foremost motivational
expert. Zig Ziglar was to me the light that was sent to give me the
vision I had overlooked in my blind pursuit of a success I could not
define. When he entered my young life and defined the boundaries

of true success, I knew I had to hitch my wagon to his philosophy or get a new wagon, because the one I was riding was not fun anymore. In the very near future, I will have the privilege of introducing this titan of hope to the masses of my motherland. In doing so I will forego the traditional introductions of a master of ceremonies and bow in reverence as the tradition of my fathers has taught me. This will be the culmination of a journey that began many years ago when he allowed me to ride on his wagon.

Who will you thank for allowing you to ride on their wagon?

_____

_____

_____

THE GUILT THAT BREAKS YOU IS THE GUILT THAT MAKES YOU

In the pursuit of fame and fortune, we chase dreams of monetary excellence with a plan of limited intelligence. Many strive to be eight-hour professionals who can one day afford the expense of buying peace of mind. In their search for the independence that would make them win the war of survival and realize their dreams, they sacrifice the very people who allowed them to dream in the first place. How long has it been since you told your bride that you love her? When was the last time you called your parents and thanked them for their effort in financing your life? Did you ever stop to ask your father-in-law if there is anything else you can do to prove that you are worthy of his beautiful daughter? The first step is to apologize to all those that have been forsaken in the quest for riches. There is a difference between wealth and riches. Riches exist when friends respect your possessions. Wealth abounds when all those around you say they are proud of you and love you. The second step is to redefine your goals and chart a new path of consistency. S. Truett Cathy, founder of Chick - Fil-A and author of the book *It is Easier to Succeed Than to Fail,* calls this process Maker – Mate – Mission.

A PRIVATE LESSON ON SUCCESS

As I prepared for one of my many trips, I saw my son who was seven sitting quietly in the corner almost crying, but using his little resolve to hold back the tears. I approached him with the gentleness of a father and a little ignorance of a busy man who had things to do and problems to solve. When I asked him to state the nature of his discomfort he sweetly acknowledged that he had no idea what I did for a living. Wanting to make a positive impression, I responded that I was a teacher and trainer and that I had plied my craft all over the world. Seeking validation from him for my choices, I narrated all the things I had supposedly accomplished that made me successful. Without batting an eyelid, Nicolas replied, "You are obviously not good enough to do it in Dallas." The reminder of the fragility of an innocent opinion and the impact of weight it bears on an already guilty soul led me to change my definition of success. Today I affirm the following to my boy:

I may never gather diamonds and gold
Others may have a differing opinion when my story is told,
But if you can grow up Godly my boy, I will be glad
For at least I know I will have been successful as your dad.

I AM ABLE TO DO WHAT I DO BECAUSE OF YOU

Sitting on the edge of the bed and contemplating another evening of loneliness, the emptiness of the moment overwhelmed me. Another presentation had just been completed and the applause for the performance had long since died. The guilt of being away from my family overcame me and I wept for my misfortune. Like most people who transverse far from their abode in search of fame and fortune, I too had come away from those I loved. At that moment of realizing my inadequacy and wondering why most of us make the same mistake, I prayed for an answer. *Typically in the search for the prize and the need for self-discovery we tell those who love us that what we do, we do for them. This guilt eats away at the performing soul in distant motel rooms and lonely airport lounges. The day you change your vocabulary your world will become easier and your performance will not require the validation of strangers. Now I always remind my family that what I do I am able to do because of them.* Now when anyone asks me where I am going, I always reply "Home - I just have to stop in Pittsburgh (or wherever I am headed) on the way." This strategy has been the formula that has forced me to remember that making speeches is what I do - it is not who I am. Anila's husband and Nicolas's father is who I am. That is all I am and always will be.

"Respect and love your wife as your father did me, and you will be amazed at your own success." Lakshmi Dhanam (my mother)

"For every step you take forward, I will take one right behind

you. If you ever fall, I will be right there to catch you. Do not be afraid to succeed." N. S. Dhanam (my father)

BUILDING WINNNING RELATIONSHIPS

Many a relationship has turbulence and some suffer more severely than others during the rough times. Anyone who claims that his relationship has been free from turmoil is either living in denial or oblivious to successful relationships built on constant effort. The likelihood of two people agreeing on everything all the time is a long shot. Compromise is when people settle for a solution when both believe they got part of what they bargained for. The experts who suggest that relationships in life are more than compromise deal with the complete journey. Again we are looking at finishing well. Like organizations that have a vision and a mission, successful relationships can be built when each partner hitches to a clearly drafted vision for the relationship.

1. Division of labor

The value of the individual parts needs to be greater than the whole for any relationship to stand the test of uncertainty. This simply means that both parties need to give more than one hundred percent to each of the tasks they have undertaken as part of their commitment. One of the things that derail relationships is the uneven distribution of effort. With the intense changes in working environments today, many homes have both adults in the home working. This leaves a certain amount of work still to be done. Common questions are: Who will pick up the kids? Who will make dinner? Who will assist with the homework? Who will get the kids ready for bed? Whose job is more important? When relationships are in this stage it is imperative that the tasks be divided and a commitment made to trust the other's performance. While some ways are more efficient than others, the premise of shared responsibility is to get the task done in a way not necessarily your way or a certain way.

What are the roles you can divide in your relationship? Are you certain you can then allow your partner to do his and her share without constantly correcting him or her?

_____

_____

_____

2. Will this affect life?

Sometimes the arguments of pettiness undermine the vows taken in front of many a worthy witness. One of the couples who attend church with us uses a simple technique to thwart some of those petty arguments from continuing- "Will this affect life?" Saying "I do" is serious business and falling-out of love more easily than falling in love is becoming a pastime that is all too prevalent. This occurrence that was purely Western is now permeating all parts of the globe as disenfranchised partners seek divorce or separation as a solution. It is imperative that we look at the future and ask ourselves if life will really be affected if a toilet seat is left up or the paper towel was put on the dispenser in an unusable way.

"There are four steps to accomplishment. Plan Purposefully, Prepare Prayerfully, Proceed Positively and Pursue Persistently." Anon.

What are some petty things that can be avoided by asking the question – "Will this affect life?"

_____

_____

_____

3. The honeymoon should never end

Most relationships set a finite number of days for the bliss to last before the drudgery of life takes over. This period is called the honeymoon. It is ironic that individuals precondition themselves to a day when the honeymoon is over. Why not plan the relationship with the goal of having a lifelong honeymoon? The trials and tribulations of life are commonplace to every relationship and, though not easy, can be weathered if the commitment is permanent. Zig Ziglar always indicates the number of years he has been married by stating the number of honeymoons he has been on. His logic is that anniversaries are boring but he has never been on a boring honeymoon. I am confident that life would be a lot simpler if people forced themselves to think of the marital journey as a never-ending honeymoon. My parents have been married for almost fifty years and my father's advice to me on relationships is as follows: "Son, treat your spouse as your biggest victory. Wake up each morning and thank yourself for the win, then spend the entire day working towards proving your worthiness of this win." I have seen my father honor my mother for every waking moment I remember. Their love for each other was amplified during the most troubled times of their lives and the result has been a honeymoon that has not ended.

What are some ways for you to treat your relationships as if you were still on your honeymoon? What will you do for your mate today that you would have done for him or her on your wedding day?

_____

_____

_____

Humbled by her poverty and saddened by her plight, our child-bride Meena will swallow many indignities in life. Mohan will relate with his family in the only way he knows how. Neither will abandon the other to whom their life, liberty and freedom were committed in front of a fire that bonded them forever. Meena's husband will sometimes take her for granted and Mohan's children might get tired of playing with the pile of rubbish in front of their dwelling, but their commitment will survive. The subservience that is their destiny will serve them well during the trials and tribulations of real struggle. The falling out of love in suburbia can be avoided except in cases where abuse and neglect are evident. Feelings in life change, but as Jim Rohn has said, day will follow night and so on. Since the beginning of time there have been the seasons of life. There has never been a situation where two days happened without a night. Troubles will end and new hope will arise.

If you look to the gurus and pundits for a solution, come prepared to make a contribution of your own. Nobody can solve your problem if you are not willing to change. It may seem simple when advice dispensing requires a seven-step aggressive approach. However simple the purveyors of solutions make it, the solutions are not easy.

In 1986 I hitched myself to a star who has been my bride of eighteen plus years. We have had our shares of difficulties. Here was my promise to her, which was inscribed on a plaque and is placed on a wall in our home, in plain sight for me to be reminded of how precious she really is.

What promise will you make to those you love?

_____

_____

_____

"Somewhere in our march towards righteousness, we as a people have determined that unless everything we do gains notoriety, it is not worthy and probably will be unappreciated. Shine the spotlight on others and watch the reflection shine on you." Krish Dhanam

V

Forty-Five Hours of Productivity
Gaining a Six-Week Edge on Your Dream

"What this power is I cannot say; all I know is that it exists and it becomes available only when a man is in that state of mind in which he knows exactly what he wants and is fully determined not to quit until he finds it." Alexander Graham Bell.

Most people who commute to work do not enjoy the drive. The traffic jams, coupled with the insanity of other drivers, force a rise in body temperature for many commuters. This is when we are at our most vulnerable. In this agitated state of not being in control we are at a receptive peak for information that is destructive and counter-productive. I am fortunate that one of the most meaningful bytes of productive information came to me from an audiocassette that was playing on an otherwise standard commute. This single tape did more for my life than the combined theoretical and academic knowledge I acquired during my MBA.

The advice on the tape was to work for one extra hour a day, if you wanted to have the deciding edge on those who competed against you. This sounded too good to be true. Is success so easy? Is that all it takes for someone to make his mark in this world? I was convinced that this was simply the emotional spin used by motivational speakers to tell their audiences what they wanted to hear. After a couple of weeks I was listening to the same tape again and this time the same information made sense to me. This was not revolutionary information for my ears only. Most people do not turn common sense into common practice. In the weeks and months that followed, I started to explore the concept of becoming this forty-five hour a week professional.

QUALIFYING FOR TOMORROW'S VICTORY TAKES PREPARATION TODAY

The lieutenant and his general boarded a train and proceeded to occupy seats opposite a beautiful girl sitting next to her grandmother. After the train pulled out of the station it entered a tunnel. In the darkness of the tunnel the entire compartment heard two sounds. One was the sweet nothingness of a kiss and the other was the resounding thud of a slap. Immediately perceptions ran rampant throughout that compartment. The General thought that his soldier had taken the kiss but wondered why grandma had slapped him. The grandmother thought that it was rude of the young man to kiss her granddaughter but was delighted that she had slapped him. The young girl found it flattering the young man thought her pretty enough to kiss but wondered why grandma had slapped him. The soldier was the only one who knew the truth. In that brief moment of opportunity he grabbed the kiss and slapped his general all at the same time. In the pursuit of fame and the search for significance we sometimes get the kisses and the slaps mixed up as well. The reason we do this is we often lack preparation for tomorrow.

SETTING THE OPPORTUNITY CLOCK

"Amateurs compete to win over their competitors. Pros compete to win over themselves."

Gerhard Gschwandtner

Daily success in a project or a process does not begin when you wake up. It begins when you make a decision on how much you are going to sleep even before you go to bed. I am by conditioning a light sleeper and six hours of rest is more than enough for me. Some people need a lot more sleep and some can do with less. Identify your specific need and then work on staying with the program. I am so conditioned to this ritual that setting the clock is a backup plan. On most occasions I am awake before the sound of the buzzer. In many a hotel I have answered the wake-up call with considerable enthusiasm. Before the introduction of automated call attendants it was always an extra bonus to hear the surprise in the voice of the night operator who had made the call to wake me up. My wake up time in most cases is around 4:00 AM. This allows me to be at work by 5:30 AM when I am not traveling. When I am traveling I still maintain the same schedule and use that time for preparation of the presentation or just getting things in order.

Over the years many people have asked me if I burn out at any point in the day or hit critical mass. I normally do this in the afternoon and use an early exit as my strategy to beat burnout. The added bonus comes in being able to beat the traffic on the commute home. My day in the office is normally from 5:30 AM to 3:00 PM. I do not believe there is any such thing as a "morning person." I believe the desire to be productive will allow you the opportunity to become whatever kind of person you want to be. I have always awakened early because I grew up watching my parents anticipate each dawn with zest and hope. The feeling of control as you wind your way through deserted streets early in the morning, knowing you are going to get a head start on the competition, is awesome. This is a feeling that can only be felt by those that practice the habits that I am talking about.

Meena and Mohan wake up early not because they choose to but because they have to. Fighting for the extra tumbler of water is part of the reward for waking up early. Having the opportunity to stumble into a maze of pollution, noise and crowded streets is the gain they get for waking up early. Struggling to get a place in the line that has already formed is the bonus that changes each day by their place in this line. Who knows? One day good fortune might see them in the front of that line. A line represented by many walks of life trying to grab a lung full of fresh air before the rituals of survival are drowned by a stampede of humanity. By contrast, some fortunate souls can wake up to the breath of freedom permeated with the possible aromas of designer coffees and cinnamon breakfasts. What a difference twelve thousand miles can make in the life of a human being. I now know why Zig Ziglar calls the alarm clock the "opportunity clock." Being Indian at heart, gratitude flows abundantly in our house when we wake up each morning in America.

REMEMBER MR. DOPA

MR.	*DO*	*PA*
Make Ready	Do	Put Away

MAKE READY

When you were hired to do your job, you officially entered into a contract with your employers to give them forty hours of productivity a week. My colleague Bryan Flanagan taught me a method many years ago, which was part of his background as National Sales Instructor for the IBM Corporation. His recommendation was to arrive at your workstation fifteen minutes before start time. If you began your day at eight o'clock, then you need to be at your desk by 7:45 AM. This process prevents you from dipping into your valuable productivity time to get the necessary preparation done. Most decisive and victorious people in life are at the site of their endeavor long before the average performer. No one wants to be like the French Legionnaire who sat up suddenly and said, "I must find out where those soldiers are marching to, for they are my men and there probably is some battle we must be fighting."

What are the many things that would make up your "make ready time"?

_____

_____

_____

_____

_____

DO

After the preparation is done and your day outlined, you need to get involved in the activities scheduled for the day. The actual doing of your job and its description involves many different elements. There is the e-mail response task, communication with colleagues on yesterday's outcomes, and the forecasting of tomorrow's needs. In addition, almost everyone has a "to do list" which they have drafted up either in the preparation stage or on the previous day. One of the important concepts that may help make your day effective is the usage of time blocks to get certain daily tasks accomplished. We have a certain number of things that we repeat. Faxing, filing, stationery retrieval, and interoffice communication are some of the activities we involve ourselves in every single day. It is advisable to generate specific time blocks to get these activities done.

Since my job entails dealing with requests and requirements of our global clientele, I choose to finish all my international e-mail, faxing, and calling before 6:45 AM. This strategy gives me two immediate benefits. The first is I am able to get to almost all of my overseas accounts in real time, except those in Australia and New Zealand. Our Southeast Asian partners all work until 9:00 PM and are accessible on their mobile numbers. The second is the ability to use fax and modem lines without interruption, as some of the exchanges for international telecommunication have special settings that take up more time than domestic transmissions.

Whatever the nature of your specific job, it is imperative that you identify key blocks of time so you can plan accordingly. Pareto's law clearly defines for us that 20% of our time is spent on activities that give us 80% of our reward. If this is true, as has been proven time and again, why don't we devote more time towards the activities that yield the highest reward? One of the stigmas that individuals have suffered in professional pursuit is not winning many office popularity contests except with management because they take their 'Do' time very seriously. On a personal note, participating in joyous activities that would take me away from tasks that are important is a chore to me. Being successful as a team player and being motivated to accomplish the mission of the organization has very little to do with being liked. In reality, the only popularity contest I want to win is the one at home. Professional rewards and accomplishments are just those, reminders of a job done well. Nevertheless, isn't the point of it all to do a good job and be the best you can be and then some? Thirteen years ago, I joined Ziglar Training Systems as a telemarketer because I fell in love with the productivity ideals of Zig Ziglar. Today they have rewarded my work ethic by allowing me to represent them as the Vice President of Training for their worldwide operations. The extra hour a day has paid off.

If you could achieve something significant by gaining an extra hour a day, what would it be?

_____

_____

_____

PA: PUT AWAY

The end of each day is usually looked upon with anticipation. It is the time when you give yourself some recognition for a job well done and look forward to what is in store for you tomorrow. Make the "put away time" start after your eight-hour commitment is done. Spend ten to fifteen minutes after your "do time" is over to wrap up your work, clean your desk and leave. Unfortunately, most offices start their "put away" at least one hour before the end of each day, losing almost five hours an employee per week. This adds up to the number one theft in the world today. It has been said the number one crime being committed on the job today is the stealing of organizational time.

Let us look at our formula. If you gave your employer sixty more minutes a day and did that five days a week, your productivity would equal that of someone who has been given six extra weeks every year. Who amongst us has not felt the need and urge to discover ways to gain more time?

This procedure is simple, but not easy. Finding the extra time to allocate to a world that is already so demanding is asking a lot. I have heard it said in many circles that 97% of the people in this world operate in the *comfort zone* and 3% of the people operate in the *effective zone. The difference between comfort and effectiveness is called growth, and growth is uncomfortable.*

Giving Your All

Sam Kamaleson an outstanding preacher from India told a story which I paraphrase. The boy had a collection of marbles that were his pride and joy. They were big and little, colorful and shiny and the envy of all the kids he played with. He had inherited most of them from his older brother who had taken good care of them. The girl had much candy and had saved her allowance every week to invest in her growing stock. She always carried a small supply to partake in during playtime but was careful to always add to her inventory because she never wanted to run out. One day the boy and the girl decided to make a deal. She would give him all her candy if he gave her all the marbles. There comes a time in all our lives when we tire of what we know and trade it for what we think someone else has that is more valuable.

The girl brought all the candy to the point of exchange and met the boy who produced his marbles. All the marbles were there except the most prized ones that had been carefully separated and hidden. The boy and the girl exchanged their glorious collections and went their separate ways. That night the girl slept blissfully as she marveled at her new possession and was thankful for her treasure. The boy lay awake wondering if she had given him all the candy or if she had held some back just like he had. Do you stay awake at night wondering if you had given it your all? Have you ever held back just enough so you had an escape hatch to crawl through when the chosen path closed before it ever revealed its promise? Whom have you bartered with in the journey of life that got less than they deserved but gave you more than they had?

Many a relationship grows stale as husbands and wives are convinced that they have given their all while secretly holding back just the right amount to sustain them in case of peril. Many a father walks away from the princess of his eyes when she transforms into the woman who someone else is going to get. He then holds back and says to himself that it really does not matter. We are all victims of this saga that convinces us that we do not need to give it our all because in the grand scheme of living no one will ever know the difference. However, the sleepless nights and restless moments do not trouble the people who did not receive your all. They usually create consternation for the one who know that he or she could have given more. In the coming days take time to give your all to the ones you love. Give more than you have to the commitments you made when you were chosen to belong. Do not only participate if you have something to spare from the abundance that you own. Willfully pledge your all to those around you and make sacrifice a priority. You will soon learn that happiness depends on happenings but the unadulterated joy of livening comes from giving your all. The attribute of successful relationships is predicated on giving your all. Many a marriage falters because somewhere in the journey we start taking each other for granted. There then comes a moment when we stand in our respective paths while expecting the others to do their part and wishing that all would be well. While knowing in some deep corner of their being that the outcome is not going to be positive. Learning that to gain friendship first requires being a friend is a key learning point this week.

1. Make an effort to corral someone this week that you know and love and care about and give them your undivided attention while focusing on solving their problems.

_____

_____

_____

2. Make a list of the opportunities you had this week to give a little more but held back because you were waiting for something that will not come.

_____

_____

_____

Comfort zone effort vs. Effective zone performance

The best-selling author of *Megatrends*, John Naisbitt, reports in his book *Global Paradox* about the congruence between integrity and the bottom line. Referring to a report to the readers in the April 1992 issue of *Industry Week*, Naisbitt quotes the magazine as follows: "They are wrong. Integrity and performance are not at the opposite ends of the continuum. When people work for an organization that they believe is fair, where everyone is willing to give, to get the job done, where traditions of loyalty and caring are hallmarks, people work to a higher level. The values around them become a part of them, and they think of the customer as someone whom they owe the finest possible product and service."

There are indeed two kinds of people striving to gain security in this world. One type relies on the security of the extended chain and focuses solely on being dependent. These people will not work anymore than they are required to. Their status quo revolves around being complacent and going with the flow. They are more susceptible to being influenced by change and transition. They are not intrinsically bad, but do have a harder time understanding organization loyalty. Their perception of forgiveness overlooks logic and they are motivated by events that lack competition and challenge. These are typically people who stay and operate in their *Comfort Zone*. While secure in their environment, these people can be classified into the following styles:

The Wizards

You do not have to be a believer in medieval times or a subscriber to sorcery to find the wizards of the twenty-first century. Most of the people who can be classified as wizards are individuals who think the only way to succeed is to win a popularity contest in life. Everything around them is self-defeating, so their remedy for reinventing the wheel is to update their magic wand and seek self-improvement in arenas where comforting one another is the main event. These people are bright and energetic but subscribe to the theory that no person is an island and survival depends on winning popularity contests all the time. Their focus is on pleasing others rather than on releasing their God given potential.

The Worker Bee

Deep within the corporate hive are groups of people who

confuse activity with accomplishment. They are historically the "go-to" people because they accept every assignment without the ability to say no. Their eagerness to please others forces them to take on mountains of work and before long they are swamped. The rallying cry is normally "Look at me. I stayed here until 7:00 PM. I am the fist one here and the last one to leave." Their primary motivation is derived from sincerity to their chosen cause and their effort is genuine. They do get stomped on because of their nature. Again they choose the comfort of the comfort zone and allow themselves to be overwhelmed. If you ever need medicine for heartburn, a migraine, a weak stomach, or any other daily ailment, go to the worker bees in your office. Their supply cabinet is always full.

The Candy Striper

Every organization has professional volunteers. They are so bored with their own role and responsibility that they spend most of their day volunteering their suggestions or offering their services in areas outside their influence. Tom Peters, the best-selling author and leadership expert, encourages boundary bashing, but the Candy Stripers take this to a level, which is sometimes unproductive. Peters encourages us to learn about other functions in our organization and encourages us to learn about other offerings in our industry. However, this should not be done at the sacrifice of your own job. I vividly remember that in my own pursuits I had to offer my services to many different parts of the organization. I, however, did not do it to just help. I did it primarily to learn, and in the process assist someone else in reaching his or her own goals. The fundamental difference between a "Boundary Basher" and a "Candy Striper" is at the end of the day the "Boundary Basher" is closer to his/her own goals. However "Candy Striper" has helped someone have a better day, but at a price that prevented them from meeting their own responsibilities. It is not my intent to diminish the process of helping in an organization. It is imperative, however, to understand that if your focus is on helping someone it must not be done to the detriment of your own responsibility.

The Bully

The role of intimidation is also a comfort-zone role. There are certain individuals who thrive on taking ownership of other people's tasks, responsibilities and benefits through intimidation. These people are normally feared within the confines of their organization more because of their ability to dominate the dialog through loud voices and other attention getting tactics. The Bully is feared by his colleagues and normally is on the winning end of many disputes. Management acknowledges them and in most cases a "let sleeping dogs lie" philosophy is in force. These people are not known to give more to their environment than it asks of them. Their whole play is built around the concept that the rules of the game are unfair and if they have to survive through intimidation then they are going to look out for themselves.

Each of the roles identified in the Comfort Zone is necessary for the survival of the company. However, we often find the people exercising the weaknesses of each role and not balancing that with the strengths associated with each role. People who live in the comfort zone will not stretch themselves, for fear of failing or being exposed to situations that might overwhelm them. Nevertheless, their survival and contribution are integral to an organization's pursuit of strategic excellence. Most managers in today unknowingly pamper their employees who are Comfort Zone people.

Just like the Comfort Zone, those who operate in the Effective Zone have strengths and weaknesses. These people thrive on chaos and more often than not create the change that causes problems. They know what it is like to be down-and-out and adopt a guerrilla warfare mentality that anything goes. They often ignore rules and many times change the rules to justify potential benefits. For these people yesterday did end last night and today is the first day of the rest of their lives. They are not bothered by the office opinion poll and are normally the focus of many of the rumors in the office. Their security lies in performance and they do not worry about qualitative measurement.

As mentioned earlier, there are a couple of different kinds of people who operate in the Effective Zone. These people are strategically closer to the head of the typical organizational pyramid and usually leave as quickly as they arrive because of the breathlessness they cause with their desired pace.

The Pole-Vaulter

Every effective zone has a couple of these types of people. They do make a big splash and the runway of their momentum looks like it is unusually long. They brag of the big deal and show all of their aces daily. Just when speculation begins to mount about their ability to deliver they produce a home run that benefits the organization. There is no silent way for these people to operate. It is inconceivable for them to do a day's work without someone commenting in awe about the preparation and dazzle of the pole-vaulter. The pole-vaulter operates in the Effective Zone and is more often than not a forty-one hour professional. His/her primary desire is to raise the bar of excellence publicly. If something is desired of them they want you to make an announcement. If they exceed they will demand recognition, but if they come up short they will admit it wholeheartedly.

The Hurdler

The Effective Zone "go to person" is the hurdler. This person is methodical in her approach and calculates the distances to the next hurdle. These are the people who seem to be prepared for any eventuality and run with determination. You will not see them participating in water cooler gossip or mid-afternoon breaks. They are considered key anchors to organizational survival and are the kinds of people who always have a project going on. Their biggest fear is being taken advantage of. The hurdler is one who is normally in line for the next promotion and is always privy to confidential information. They may not be the key decision-makers but have access to information based on their approach to role and responsibility.

The Tiger

An organized bully is referred to as a tiger. Most organizations have their tigers in the sales departments. These people are crafty and operate under a tremendous amount of pressure. They are deadline conscious and acknowledge survival of the fittest. They are always there, lurking in the background. They sense weakness and pounce for the kill at the most opportune time. Their strategy of operation is simple, be prepared, have all skills sharp, wait for the opportunity and take advantage the moment it is possible.

Which of these roles do you identify with? If you are a combination of more than one of the roles listed above, what are the strengths you want to recognize and what are the weaknesses in those roles that you would like to eliminate?

Strengths

_____
_____
_____

Weaknesses

_____
_____
_____

The different kinds of people who walk the halls of the modern organization make some sort of contribution. Most of the contributions can be determined as positive or negative, but they are all contributions nonetheless. However, as we look back over time and chart success in the twenty-first century, we will notice that most of the great people of our time came out of the Effective Zone. In order for the future to be bright and for the shining stars of tomorrow to have a chance, we need to encourage the youth of today to do a little more. The battle cry of every company seeking profitability as a mission should be demanding a little more from everyone. This might be easier said than done. How will you communicate to the underdogs of today that if they want to be champions tomorrow they have to give more of themselves without any guarantee of gain? The questions of survival are the toughest ones we will ever answer.

The questions about the glass ceiling and unbreakable barriers are tougher than those of increased productivity and enhanced morale. Tell a young college graduate about showing up early and leaving late and he will ask you if there are any guarantees. Convince him or her about the loyalty needed for survival and they will show you a genealogy of loyal family members who were trampled under the rug of supremely colored ignorance. Ask the young immigrant mother who just came from another country if she would like to be a forty-five hour professional and she will show you many in her neighborhood that worked longer, strove harder and received less. Ask the young Indian immigrant who is working the graveyard shift in the convenience store about his prospects in 21st Century America and his answers will be similar to those of his predecessors, two decades ago. "I am going to be a doctor, an engineer, or own a motel." Just kidding!

To Meena the "Effective Zone" is the wit and charm required daily. From beneath the squalor of subservient living, dreams ravaged by the uncertainty of the slum she lives in, she forges the last remnants of a smile for her man. Mohan grimaces as the blister on his foot tears and the heat of the asphalt shoots pain through the sole as flesh comes in contact with another harsh element. Nevertheless, he cannot stop. He has to be effective for his family and find another fare. Soon the monsoons will be here and the flooding will bring other problems. The blister of today pales in comparison to what he is yet to face.

Shorten the stick, sweeten the carrot and give the donkey a bite

One of the famous cartoons of yesteryear is the one of the donkey with a carrot in front of it on a long stick, and a burden on its back that is more than it can carry. The simple message in the illustration is if the donkey is hungry enough, it will tote the load. Organizations have demanded productivity from their employees for hundreds of years using the incentive motivation illusion portrayed in this cartoon. The problem with incentive-oriented thinking is that after some time very few continue to thrive under this illusion. A vast majority concede defeat, and do not even suit up for the race every time an incentive laden competition is announced.

There are many classes of people who believe that across-the-board competition is unfair. These people are quick to insult the notion that everyone has to do more just to survive, while the greedy corporate executives continue to drive nice cars, live in good homes, and take exotic vacations. They see themselves as the donkey with the load and the carrot ever so slightly out of their reach.

In schools across the globe, testing patterns are being challenged as being discriminatory and unfair. One group wants bilingual education and demands so because in the very near future

135

they will be a majority in California and maybe soon after in Texas. Another group believes that centuries of oppression and racism have prevented them from learning and thus we need to adjust the test scores to give everybody a level playing field. The debate will be endless. Corporate executives are sending their employees to Diversity Training, Sensitivity Training, Stress Reduction Training, Assimilation Training, and Team Building Training. How about training on showing up for work at 8:00 AM and not whining about the traffic, and every other inconvenience of modern day living? The day I hear an employee walk into a boss's office and say, "I am grateful for air-conditioning and indoor plumbing," is the day I will become compassionate to the overworked and underpaid masses. Is it any wonder that productivity across-the-board is increasingly becoming a dream of overly ambitious people who want to run successful companies into the 21st century and beyond?

The world needs to wake up and smell the horizon of defeat before the vanquished of today lower the bar of mediocrity. There is more to survival than watching re-runs of longhaired gypsy singers humming tunes saying, "I got you babe." I am not a critic by any stretch of the imagination, just someone confused by the lowering of standards. Inequality and inequity are the forces that make the economies of the world operate. On a recent business trip to India, I interviewed some folks who work for a company that has catapulted to the forefront of global enterprise. Many of them work more than twelve hours a day and are so grateful for the privilege of work that it is hard to tell where the real motivation comes from. These are the people doing the jobs that someone sent to them because they do it for less, and do it with dignity. I am outraged when someone loses a job in America because the job is outsourced. I live in America and hurt if the economy hurts in America. However, I am encouraged by the resilience of the human spirit all over the world. By contrast, Meena and Mohan will never have their roles outsourced. I can well imagine an evening newscast saying that pulling rickshaws has become so popular in San Francisco that Mohan is leading a march in Kolkata to protest the moving of his job to America.

The benefits of productivity

Dr. Merrill Douglass of the Time Management Center in Marietta, Georgia, says that good planners consistently get better results than poor planners do. His focus on the difference between success and failure is a couple of hours each day that an individual can find by effective planning.

According to Dr. Douglass, time planning involves answering four simple questions:

1. What do I want to accomplish?
2. What activities must be done to accomplish it?
3. What are the priorities involved?
4. How much time will each activity require?

Yet another way to look at the benefits of planning your time and controlling your productivity is scheduling blocks of time for all the important outputs in your day. If you could categorize the different things you do everyday and apportion a block of time for each of those activities, you would be more productive and more in control.

Examples of blocks of time are:

SUPERIOR TIME: The time required by your immediate supervisor, or any other person on that level in the organization hierarchy.

CO-WORKER TIME: Time required by people on the same level in the hierarchy as you.

PEER TIME: Time required by colleagues who are more friends than actual beneficiaries or requisites to your workflow.

PERSONAL TIME: Time for yourself that is work related and job related and required by you to keep yourself organized and up to date.

RECREATIONAL TIME: Time to relax and ease some of the pressures of working.

EDUCATIONAL TIME: Time devoted to learning new ideas and concepts that will help you grow mentally and emotionally.

SPIRITUAL TIME: Time for reflection and healing that allows you to cleanse yourself of all that is negative so you can have inner happiness and joy.

RELAXATION TIME: Time spent with those you love focusing

on who you are, not what you do.

DRIVE TIME: Commuter time that allows you the rare opportunity to enroll in Automobile University and increase your knowledge and wisdom.

MAKE READY TIME: The time utilized at the start of each day when you plan, prioritize and establish all other blocks of time.

By adhering to a system of blocking your time you now have the opportunity to do what is needed in each one of those blocks. Like any rationing system you need to ration your time. Your superior may not want to see you every day, but if you have allocated an hour to him and her every day then at the end of the week you have allocated five hours to meet his or her needs. If they do not use their allotted time, focus on performing activities during that time like filing, memo-writing, miscellaneous paperwork, etc. This gives you the flexibility to be interrupted by the designate of that specific block of time.

In so many scenarios you see the wasting of time by people who gather to plan the birthday party, complete with the likes and dislikes of each attendee's preference and flavor of the icing on the proverbial cake. They will also follow with infinite caution the trail of the birthday card for fear of loss of the greetings. They will demonstrate all the skills of time management in petty, mundane activities and panic the moment you ask them to record their daily sales calls.

Zig Ziglar suggests doing the following activity for a week to track your use of your time. He suggests that we go as far as breaking up each hour of productivity into five-minute slots and recording what we did in every five-minute slot of a working day. The revelations will, he says, be startling as we find out how much time we waste. I was surprised when I heard the biggest time wasters are those under the age of thirty. The reasoning is the inability of a younger mind to stay focused, and the ease with which their mind wanders to things they perceive as important. One great spectacle you can witness every day in the reception areas of companies is the infamous lunch exodus. They know where they are going, whose car they are taking, the specific dish they are going to order, and the tip they are going to leave. Yet simple project management techniques that require time management become an enigma. The reason is not because the task is difficult but because the tasks that need to be done might be prioritized as mundane.

The younger generation of this country is unconvinced of the merits of personal productivity. They grow up detesting the possibility of war, and with shaven heads, ill-fitting clothes, and dull vocabularies they march the march of self-righteousness. They are convinced that productivity is a myth and reward for an honest day's work is a beeper, a cell phone, designer clothes, and the incessant need to fit into groups that do not want them as members. They arrive at the line of employment with a preconditioned stigma that they are not going to have enough. They are right in their perception and hence fulfill the legacy of ignorance. The bill of rights that gives us all the right to work is the same bill of rights that allows people in this country free speech. It is ironic, though, that the ones who complain about their inability to understand the store clerk's accent can somehow understand the same accent when it is by an Indian doctor.

On the other hand, Mohan the rickshaw driver plans his day meticulously. If he does not get to the bus station at noon, the blazing heat and scorching asphalt will be all he gets today. The businessman who comes in on the noon bus and wants to be transported to the main bazaar will find another rickshaw driver if Mohan is not ready, willing, and able to do his job. To escape the heat the businessman might give Mohan an extra two rupees as a tip. This would be the equivalent of a nickel and Mohan does not want to miss out on it. He plans and he prepares to be there when the bus comes in. He will run to the door of the bus and lunge or grab at the briefcase of anyone who looks like he might need a rickshaw ride. His two daughters hope that their dad will get a tip today so those beautiful plastic beads they saw with the street vendor might now be theirs. This is the personal productivity of a poor man who can never afford the luxury of a planner and never witness the wealth of time management. However, he has more control over his day than most people with a regular job, an air-conditioned office, working telephones and a country that protects their survival.

"In a world gone crazy and a society gone lazy, thank you America for embracing the legal immigrants. Just let your people keep complaining about their feelings of injustice. Before the complainers figure out the definition of the wrong that they accuse you of, the immigrants will move closer to their respective American dreams. Keep complaining, America, there is more for us to do." Krish Dhanam

VI

You Can Too

The World can be Your Oyster

Success...seems to be connected with action. Successful men keep moving. They make mistakes, but they do not quit. Conrad Hilton

It was February and the chill in the air reminded us of the cold days of communism and the path of hopelessness left behind by the crumbled Soviet Empire. Standing behind a stained glass window in the heart of the Mathias Chapel, two excited souls gazed in wonder at the expanse of beauty in front of them. This was the new Hungary. A baby gazing at her own future while the comforter of discontent was finally removed. Richard called out to me and said, "Bubba, go stand over there so I can take your picture, and when I'm done you can take one of me, too." Our childish innocence permeated the scenery of beauty as we looked at the mighty Danube and the history it separated as it flowed through the heart of Budapest. Eleven hundred years of existence saw this small Eastern European nation face occupation from Rome, Austria, Turkey and Russia. At the height of popularity of the Ottoman Empire, the very chapel we stood in was a mosque for a hundred and fifty years.

The town of Budapest and the architectural brilliance of its history are reminders of how small our world really is. As we stood there gazing at the beauty of a resurrected city, we smiled at our own fortune. In our individual pursuits as people we have traveled to many places. Nevertheless, when we looked at where we were, we marveled at the moment and then gushed at our accomplishment. I must confess as I write this that I feel a sense of accomplishment to have seen so much of the free world. To witness such splendor as the mist settling on Lake Balaton and to have traveled to the Czech border and seen the demolished bridge that defied Russia is a grand feeling. To have shared it with someone to whom I owe more than my triumphs is splendid. It is said friendship can stand any test if it is built on respect and laced with admiration. The leaders of this world all demand respect and entire generations of freethinkers ignore those demands. The reason for corporate mediocrity is the abundance of false respect and the absence of genuine admiration. You cannot perform under directive if your performance is inhibited by disbelief in the leader.

What are some of the beliefs you have about the leaders you follow?

_____

_____

_____

What are some things you are grateful for, and why are you grateful for them?

What	Why

I am Sure I Can Salvage Him

Sometimes in life opportunities present themselves in shabby disguises. Looking past the weathered exterior into the heart of a performer is critical to finding the truth. The time seems so long ago and the place seems so far away, but the haunting memory of lost self-esteem and the award of a defeated ego make it more recent. While the innocence or guilt of my actions seems moot at this point, I will never vindicate myself completely from some of the responsibility of that phase in my life. I will remember that day as if it were yesterday. Self-doubt and self-pity were the highlights of the day in question. My career was almost finished when the organization I had represented for so many years gave me another chance. "I am sure we can salvage him," were the words of assurance given by one of my superiors, Richard Oates, to those wondering why I had been given another chance. In this sometimes confusing journey we call life I had found an entity that believed in me for whom I was and not what I had supposedly done. Those were the best of times and amidst the deep resentment caused by the shame and humiliation of professional failure, I found a home. The price I paid was a pittance for the reward I have received in the subsequent journey.

Looking at your journey who can you credit for believing in you?

If you cannot think of someone, become someone who can believe in others.

Goals are Dreams with Feet

President John F. Kennedy once asked a nation to come together and have a common goal of putting a man on the moon. Mahatma Gandhi asked for nonviolence as the means to humble the imperialist armies of Great Britain. In the US and in India the followers of those dreams credit the visionaries for the ensuing success as America successfully achieved lunar supremacy and India gained freedom after two hundred years of colonial rule. I am convinced that people with a vision have a better chance of putting feet to their dreams. Solomon said that his people perished for a lack of a vision. When Saul was on his road to Damascus it was the anointing by the Lord that gave him a new vision to further the gospel. It is not only appropriate for every individual to look at the road ahead, but a must to have the plans that will bear fruit in the future.

"When you're in focus, your life takes on a new clarity. Just as a camera lens focuses light to form a photographic image, so your mind focuses your thoughts, feelings and actions to form a clear picture of who you are and where you are going." Nido R. Qubein

On a recent trip to Milwaukee, I was reminded about the power of dreaming and the benefits of a vision. Mr. Ziglar was speaking to one of our major corporate clients. I was accompanying him on the trip because I had personally been involved in the development of the sales training program and the ensuing train the trainer sessions that were conducted. In addition, many of the regions had utilized my services as a keynote speaker at various kick-off events during the past three years. The joy I felt at being recognized by so many independent businessmen and their families overwhelmed me. I remember some of them bragging on me to Mr. Ziglar at the fine job I had done in representing him and his core philosophy. I was equally overjoyed when Mr. Ziglar reminded those that had made the comments that true joy for the teacher is when the student receives accolades.

Incredible Iceland

The Nordic ancestry of a small island that sits at the cusp of the Arctic Circle narrates the richness of the sagas of old. The vastness of this lava bed and the majesty of its uneven topography are the beauty that is Iceland. Who would have ever thought that one day I would be fortunate enough to conduct a seminar on sales and facilitate one on customer service in this last frontier? I fell in love with Iceland's breathtaking beauty the day I arrived. The simplicity of nature combined with the uninterrupted conveniences of modern living make this island a hidden paradise. This country with less than a quarter of a million inhabitants boasts of the highest per-capita literacy rate in the world and the longest life expectancy of any country in the world. Despite torrential arctic blizzards and howling winds, the warmth of the souls of these common people gives them the pride and dignity to survive. Their friendliness and hospitality surpasses many and their inherent happiness is a testimony to satisfaction in what they have.

Amidst the splendor of rolling hills and the geological instability of bubbling geysers, you can find a peace in Iceland that is tranquil and serene. Whether we were sitting in a coffee shop listening to seasoned sailors debate politics, or eating salmon in an award-winning restaurant, we found a peace among the people. This peace emanated from a fundamental pride in their roots and an insatiable honor in their legacy. As I sat in the geothermal spa known simply a "Blue Lagoon," I wept for my own success because I know of many who are a part of my roots who would never see such joy or feel such peace.

Nowhere in the sub-continent of India could Meena or Mohan find this beauty. As I write these words, I pray that all of you can one-day dream to see the world, wake up from the dream, and find yourself in the heart of beauty enjoying the most incredible parts of creation. In a doubtful yet happy way I now know why it is said that beauty is in the eye of the beholder. If those that could see the wonders of God's creations paused to consider the options He has given us, we might be less inclined to butcher each other's dreams and destinies. Iceland was a reminder of the cataclysmic coming together of nature and belief. Look around you and ask yourself what would be incredible for you to see. Set a goal, chart a course, and conquer the destinations of your imaginative mind.

The following steps will assist you in realizing your own potential and following through on your dreams:

1. **Set Goals to Change**

Goal achievement is for those who have an arsenal of previously qualified goals that are categorized as those you want to achieve in the short-term and the lofty long-range goals that might take you three or more years to attain. The bottom line is that to achieve something of significance, you have to qualify it, sort it, write it, work on it, and only then will you achieve it.

A goal setting process to foster change begins with **identifying your goal** and **listing the benefits** you would gain from accomplishing it. Remember the more personal you make the benefits, the more motivated you will be to accomplish your goal. Once that is done you need to **isolate the obstacles** that would prevent you from reaching the goal, and **identify the skills or knowledge** that will give you the momentum you need to succeed. It is vital that when you are moving from point A to point B in life, you need to learn what is required at point B while still at point A. This method enables you to arrive at your chosen destination more prepared and better equipped to handle whatever is thrown your way.

The next phase in goal achievement is **locating the influencers** who can assist you. The good book says that the strong and wise admit they are weak. Seeking the counsel of those that are already proven winners in a given field will enable you to be more prepared as you **detail your personal plan of action** and **set a completion date**. Using this simple process and having a daily disciplinarian to aid you will move you from the majority of the population who are in the comfort zone to the few who are in the effective zone.

What have you dreamt about that can become a reality for you?

_____

_____

_____

2. Expand your circle of TRUST

In our hurry to move from dependence to independence, we have abandoned the closeness that comes from trust. Families have fragmented and independence in thought, action and guilt have become the order of the day. It is a misfortune to see most of the civilized world walking along in cocoons of individuality with no love, ambition or vision to share with others. We have become so accustomed to sinister messages of conspiracy that we have lost the innocence and pleasure that come from trust.

"Other people will give you pleasure, but you will never discover true happiness until you do something for someone else." Zig Ziglar.

When the race of life is run, the victors are not those who ran well but those that finished well. Winning in all areas of life requires celebrating the victories with those that mean the most to you. Therapy might give you closure to past indiscretions committed by those you trusted, but true happiness will come from forgiving those people as you would like to be forgiven for your own errors.

3. Increase your tolerance for pain

When there are changes in the economy out there, look at what is a weakness within you that needs to be overcome and put a plan of action in place so you can make that weakness into strength. Edwin Moses, who is undoubtedly one of the best middle distance runners of all-time, was an active advocate of this principle. His streak of victories at one time was over a hundred consecutive races and spanned almost a decade. When asked about his motivation for such peak performance, he replied that he had a higher threshold of pain than many of his competitors. Taking a weakness like pain and making it into strength by focusing on having a higher breaking point is what separated him from the others. Many of us do get hurt and fall down. We only fail if we stay there or do not learn anything from the failure. Zig Ziglar says that people do not drown by falling into water, they only drown if they stay there.

What are some of the perceived agonies in your life that cripple you and prevent you from moving forward?

_____
_____
_____

How will you stretch your tolerance level in these situations?

_____

_____

_____

4. Your self-worth is more than any economy can pay you

Regardless of the times, in most places of work the wage earning process is simple. For the first two weeks a person works, he does not accomplish anything of significance because he is on a learning ramp. Miraculously he gets paid. The next two weeks' performance moves to marginal at best and he gets paid again. For four whole weeks the individual in question has not even hit stride, but the employer by law is required to compensate him twice. This leads to expectancy in the minds of the working populace of the world they are owed something. Performance based on what others think you are worth because they pay you for it leads to mediocrity. If you reverse the equation, your self-worth increases. Imagine that someone is paying you twice so you can learn more than you know and become more valuable to the enterprise you are a member of. This forces individuals to perform on the premise of gratitude, which is a healthier and more productive emotion than regret or greed.

"It is better to light a single candle than curse the darkness."
Motto of the Christophers.

Redefine your self-worth based on what you are grateful for.

_____

_____

_____

I do believe that true success is not measured by how much you accumulate but by how much the world wanted you to be a part of it. As I traverse this beautiful world we live in, and share the memories of promise with some of the most talented people I know, the lessons I am taught prove to be my biggest asset. As the passport of my adopted home has page after page stamped with jubilation of yet another destination, the blessing that is the varied world that we live in overwhelms me.

Mohan mops his brow and stoops down in front of the trickle of water and smiles. The water is cool and his physical thirst is quenched. His emotional thirst of hopes and dreams for his daughters will never be quenched. His life will run parallel to the spinning of the wheels of his rickshaw and at the end of his journey of many miles he will wash his callused feet and hope he can do it again tomorrow. Meena the housewife will gladly wait for tomorrow when she can enter the arena of honor and respect and wonder if the same God that created America is the one that blessed her to have this life. What an amazing coincidence of struggle for survival and success. In the vanquished depths of indecent third world living there are many that will not see the world and will not be ignorant for they are too poor to afford ignorance. These people need a reminder that their simplicity actually lends beauty to a confused and egotistical populace that chases debauchery and indecency with rapidness.

I Remember When all I Wanted was Change

As the seasons of my youth turned the innocence of childhood dreams into an obsession of adult want, I realized I would never be satisfied until I came to America. I had arrived at a crossroads in my life where I was in love with another country and deep resentment and contempt were the feelings I had towards my own homeland. We all go through that phase when all we want is something other than that which we have. However, because of strong parental influence, I started doing something that would come back to assist me later in life when I needed it the most. I began to focus my learning towards American history and spent my time studying the cultural nuances that made it such a popular destination. The principle is very simple. If you are at Point A and want to be at Point B do not wait until you get to Point B to figure out what you need to survive and thrive there. Do the planning and preparation before you can expect the success you want for yourself. When you arrive at Point B you can exercise the skill if required. If not, you have lived with purpose and are overqualified and that is not a bad thing.

The Dream Manifested

On July 26, 1998, I parked my car alongside a curb in front of a small house in Winterset, Iowa. I was at the birthplace of Marion Michael Morisson, a.k.a. John Wayne. My bride reminded my son (who was almost five years old then) that this was indeed an important moment for dad. It was from where I stood that this portrayer of patriotism began his seventy-two year odyssey into the hearts, hopes, and minds of countless people. He was not a rocker or a swinger so he probably would not have made the cut today. From the rifle he used in the movies to the eye patch that saw him win an Oscar, the memorabilia were all there splashing grandeur across the room as if this icon still walked tall. I then realized that many people have been called legends since. However John Wayne will always be the true meaning of America and the reason pilgrims like me made the pilgrimage to this last bastion of hopes and dreams.

I could not help but shed a tear as I recalled the chases from "Hatari" and the larger than life image in the "Sands of Iwo Jima." The one-handed cocking of the rifle of righteousness in "True Grit" and the leading of fellow troops in "Green Beret" brought back memories of the America I wanted that I now had. There I was where he began. From there you could go anywhere and the furthest distance is no more than twelve thousand miles. From a nondescript house in the center of Winterset, Iowa, the great American icon began his journey.

How far do you think you can go? How much do you think you can achieve? Where and to whom were you born? Do you believe in your rightful inheritance? What are the sights and sounds of the future you want for yourself?

_____

_____

_____

_____

_____

_____

Lessons I Taught My Father

A most "unusual subheading in this book" is what the typical response would be to anyone who reads this. It would almost be blasphemous for any of us to consider there are things that we could teach our parents. However, before I offend anyone further let me come clean and confess that I am writing this on behalf of my son Nicolas, who has taught me many valuable lessons through his innocent observations. As a traveling dad who has packed way too many garment bags and logged countless miles, I have concluded that learning the following lessons from my boy has been a good thing.

1. **Understanding constructive criticism** – Nicolas says that the only criticism one should worry about is the constructive kind for that comes out of love. The world that pays me to ply my craft has earned the right to criticize my professional output for the profit and loss exchange that is in business is justified in its own checks and balances. However, the ones at home seem to pay a heavier price than most-yet we shrug off their criticism because it is not professional.

2. **Relax and enjoy the sunrise** – Nicolas says there is a new sunrise every day and marveling at the newness with wonderment and amazement will renew your spirit. Looking out at creation and gazing at each new wave while shrieking with delight when the cold waters touch your skin is a joy that should never be lost.

3. **Do not rush the waiter for your check** – Nicolas contends that a meal shared with the ones we love has to be savored.

This includes the whole experience from learning about the specials to sharing a single dessert because if everyone had their own that would be fattening. Sometimes we need to be asked by the waiter for we have paid the check and are still laughing as a family with no distinct agenda for the rest of the day.

While vacationing with my family in San Jose Del Cabo, I was reminded by my boy of the moments I have squandered in my haste. Learn from your loved ones as their intent is more pure than your boss' memo and the next dinner you have to take that client to. Learn to listen to the least likely sources for information and wisdom that will change your outlook. As we program ourselves to follow the path of a career or live out the promises of a vow stop ever so often and ask yourself if you are doing justice to all concerned. Many of the choices you make in your life will be reactionary. Try to savor those blessings that are in your inner circle. In a slow and calculated way each week make sure that some of the choices you make and chances you take are responsive to the needs of those closest to you.

1. As you drive your kids around this week, ask questions about their life. If something significant is happening in their life slow down and record it.

_____

_____

_____

2. What will you specifically ask your family or significant other this week when you sit down to eat your meal?

Remember to do it as a deliberate effort to know and not as an afterthought.

_____

_____

_____

Everywhere I go I am reminded of how fortunate I am to live in America, and everywhere I go in America I am shown signs of what relativism has done to the hopes and dreams of an entire generation. The absolutes of the American dream have now been categorized into bipartisan sound bytes on the steps of any landmark that would make a good backdrop. I gave myself to America many years ago with fear and trepidation. Now America is being given to India with fear and trepidation. This cycle will go on and the only thing we can do is to be prepared to take advantage of the opportunities that present themselves to us.

"If a man knows not what harbor he seeks, any wind is the right wind." Seneca

VII

The Privilege of Work

"Whatever course you have chosen for yourself, it will not be a chore but an adventure if you bring to it a sense of the glory of surviving – if your sights are set far above the merely secure and mediocre." David Sarnoff

The melodrama that provides the backdrop for the morning in most households is humorous and interesting to watch. In a fantasy world there would be the smell of cinnamon permeating the air and the music of violins would greet this new day that the Lord has made. In the real world the sounds we hear are more akin to the gurgling of depression and the burping of dissent. Every morning across the fruited plain, people rise to greet the rays of a new sun with darkened enthusiasm and gray hope. Shaded into their subconscious is the disappointment of yesterday, and the knowledge that tomorrow will be the same after another failure today. How different would it be if everyone awoke, walked out, inhaled deeply and said, "Today I am free to choose what I do and how effectively I do it. If I find my skill set less than adequate for what I want to become, I have the freedom to choose additional skills to become the person I need to be. Thank God for today. Thank God that I am one of the privileged in this world who is allowed to make choices." An affirmation like this would give people a reasonably good chance to succeed. By contrast, Mohan wakes to the stench of an overflowing river of refuse that he has to trudge through to survive. Meena combs her hair one more time and wipes the beads of sweat on her forehead with the tip of her tattered sari. She readies herself for the swarm of mosquitoes that will buzz alongside her as both of them search for an escape from the tropical heat.

HAPPINESS IS A CHOICE

The belief that needs to exist in the heart and mind of everyone is that work is not a necessity but a choice. The Bible calls work a privilege. The steps that need to be taken to ensure this belief are fairly easy.

1. Work is a privilege

There was a time early in my ascent in the corporate world where I had failed in the management of a project. I was reminded by the powers to be that my choices had indeed brought about financial hardships to the company. I was angry at the accusations and was keen on pointing fingers to implicate the others who may have been closer to the source of the actual problem. The decisions of the leadership team included making steep adjustments to my compensation package and changing my corporate identity in terms of what my title would be and where I would sit in the office. One of the calls I made to seek guidance was to my father. He queried me as to whether my consternation had ever spilled over into the realm of saying negative things about my employer. When I replied that I had done no such thing he told me that work was and always should be treated as a privilege. For as long as I had that attitude about my work I would constantly be happy in the choices I made regardless of the obstacles others would place in my path. Eventually almost a dozen years after that incident, I have made amends with all the people involved in that part of my past and have earned great accolades about my attitude during that time. Growing up in India at a time when gainful employment was a difficult endeavor, I learned some valuable lessons that seem to allow me to succeed in the West. Like Mohan and Meena my gratitude bucket continues to overflow with a low threshold of want and need. Looking ahead ask yourself as to how much you actually need to be satisfied in your work. You will quickly realize that the frivolity of our wants and needs actually make us look at work as a chore instead of as a privilege.

The question to ask yourself is whether you can look at the reasons for why you work like an architect who is about to build a building. An architect who sees a hole in the ground can correctly guess how tall the building is going to be that would fit in that hole. He is banking his reputation and staking his expertise on the size of the foundation that could fit in the hole. When you look at the depth of your soul, how big a foundation do you think you can fit in that space? Your answer will tell you a lot about your pain threshold in this life. Most people aim low and hit because their foundation is too small. When you have a solid foundation you can aim high, miss, and hit many other things along the way. Working unconditionally as if it were a privilege in a selfish and transitional culture takes more courage than you think.

2. Performing at a level higher than was requested

Meena and Mohan seem to do more with their life in India amidst hostile conditions and deplorable situations. Yet they know that they have to outperform their respective competition just to survive. Mohan must weather the monsoon and the tropical heat or some other harsh element of mother- nature just to survive. In the land of the free and the home of the brave I have witnessed a country whose ideals were built on the premise of accomplishment. The greatest generation left a landscape of possibility using the notion of doing more than you were asked to do. Yet modernity coupled with convenience seems to have convinced the people of this great land that rights matter more than responsibility. When the rally cry is seeking of advances and promises of raises before one even attempt's to do more then the bar of mediocrity begins to become the benchmark of futility. I watched my father work hard every day of his life and he felt that he needed to do more than anyone else just to break-even. This was not an indictment on societies' ability to be fair. It was a personal decision to outperform the competition every single day so that when decisions were made about employment and employability your productivity allowed you to always be secure.

The generations coming up behind us have been spectators for most of their childhood. The activities that keep them involved in the hours after school do help them a lot, but the frustration that most parents go through to make all those activities and a well-rounded child leave much to be desired. As a result we see children whose threshold for motivation is very high and impatience for reward is very low. When they enter the workforce they do not understand the concept of delayed gratification and for the first time we have increasingly creative and extremely bright workers who do not know the joy of personal stimulation to excel. They assume the status-quo will always be favorable to them and get frustrated when anyone changes the rules in the name of prosperity or capitalism. India as a thriving economy in the last decade has assumed some of this attitude in some sectors where gainful employment is guaranteed so loyalty has to be bought.

3. Great opportunity does come to those who wait

When I began working in the West, I used to experience frustration at that amount of time it took to finish certain tasks. A colleague shared about great empires having not been built in a day and that anything that was worth accomplishing would require patience. He even added that if I were to look at the finality of the accomplishment a little less and look at what was required in the short-term a little more then I would find peace. In the pursuit of happiness people should realize that in the long-run those that time their victory by carefully seeking excellence every step of the way would be the ultimate victors. The story told by Zig Ziglar about the life and pursuit of David Lofchick is an incredible reminder to all. David was born to Bernie and Elaine Lofchick and was eventually diagnosed with cerebral palsy. The Lofchicks were told that their son would always be a "spastic" but they devoted their lives to making sure their boy would lead a normal and productive life. They underwent immense hardships and had to exhibit tough love in the short term so their boy would have a lifetime of promise. They overcame the odds, defied the doubters, and engineered the turnaround of the life of their son. There was a time when this little child struggled to do one single push-up. The painstaking parental sacrifice of the moment yielded an incredible child – and later adult - filled with dreams, hopes, ambition and desire. The experts said he would not walk and he skated; they said he would not stand, and he played golf; they said he would not be normal, and he outperformed the generic definition of normalcy.

4. There is no guarantee of where you will sit

The idea that your geographic placement in a place of business is based on your tenure or longevity with an organization is an idea that will guarantee you disappointment. Even though America is a very generous country at times it can be harsh to its citizenry. However no place else on the planet assures you a second chance like this amazing nation. Most people take this assurance and debate their deserving a second chance all the way to the highest office that will listen. Many of my co-workers and residents of the place called "work" tease me as to how much they would prefer my given space with its scenic window for I am not there enough to enjoy it. In his best-selling book *Good to Great* Jim Collins emphasizes that the people who make the best executives are those who are humble. They are not overwhelming personalities, but are avid listeners and they are careful to give credit to other people. Sometimes it is hard to forget the many people in my professional life who were asked to quit their employment because their physical position in an office became the basis for their demands.

5. Raise people behind on you and ride to the top on their shoulders

The good book said a longtime ago that you need to do unto others as you would like have done unto yourself. Regardless of your socio-economic status in life helping others accomplish something will compress the space between your own past and your immediate present. This random gesture will allow those you lift up to carry you to the finish line on their shoulders. The rule is to participate in the act of assistance without a desire for compensation because it needs to be a philosophy of life not a tactic for advancement. The best way to ensure success in this world is to invest in the attributes of loyalty and gratitude while embracing the components of a good work ethic. Place less blame on those that you think owe you something and place more responsibility on your able-bodied shoulders. Praise those around you who give you a chance and seek blessings from those before you who paved the way. Most importantly leave something behind for those that come behind you to make it easier on someone else.

Whom will you offer a helping hand to this week so they may have it a little easier than you did when you began your pursuit of the dream?

_____

_____

_____

The Ritual of Work

Mohan our Indian rickshaw driver has a daily ritual. Every morning he rises at the crack of dawn. He walks to the faucet at the end of his street and takes his place in line. Wearing a loincloth to hide his despair, one can only see the protruding ribs to know that he is under nourished and overworked. Pay would be good. Minimum wage would be nice. The heated debate amongst the poor waiting for the water of hope from the faucet of dependence is at best simple. He hopes they keep the water running until at least seven that morning, for he needs to wash the tar off his feet. His daily ritual is the same. His energy bar is a piece of unleavened bread that he soaks in his cup of watered-down tea. The tea has been made from the dregs of yesterday's consumption. He wishes for the day that India would have an inner-city housing project. The roof of contentment will replace the plastic shield that keeps the rains of today out of his home. The infestation of rats and the degradation of the slum will at least be a place they can call home. Now every night he prays that the municipality will not force them to leave the slum where they illegally squat.

Before he leaves his dwelling, he surveys his assets. His net worth is primarily human and consists of a bride and two daughters who call him the provider. The daughters sleep a little longer, and he hopes they do for he wants them to have more bliss in the ignorance that comes from dreaming. He tells his bride that today will be good. He has done the ritual of cleaning his rickshaw. He has said his prayers and has rung the polished bell seven times for good luck. He has to see a businessman about a regular route. This will mean some guaranteed work. It is hot and the humidity will be unbearable, but maybe this weekend they can all go to the beach and even buy a plastic doll for their daughters. His bride smiles at him and says that she will say a special prayer for him. He will not be able to buy his lunch, so his bride packs him a raw onion and another piece of unleavened bread. The pungent juices from the onion will make the dryness of the bread go away and cater to the hunger pangs that are sure to come with the midday heat.

Mohan has a ritual. One that says if the luck of the draw came his way, the closest Mohan would come to experiencing the privilege of America would be getting a DVD of the land of the free and the home of the brave. But wait, he will first have to buy a TV and then a DVD player. Does he want this or a small wedding for his two daughters? Mohan cannot afford a choice. He is stuck with his raw onion and unleavened bread. His work will take him back to the streets of Kolkatta and his ritual will continue to be the same. He is happy in what he knows and chooses to leave unhappiness to those who have everything but still want more.

This is the India that taught me the importance of having a good work ethic. If there is hot water in the morning, I believe I am blessed. If there is a car to drive, God has spoken, and if my air-conditioner works on the way to work, look out world. As I travel around this globe and tell people that this is the simplicity required for professional excellence, the message moves some of the audience and others become guilty from the suggestions. However, no media has made it to my door asking me to clarify this insane notion that work is a privilege, not a right. When will people wake up and answer their own questions? When will they stop depending on someone to give them clarity of vision? In a world gone blind with expectation, man's biggest fallacy is using his available sight to stare into emptiness.

Asking the world to stop and look at your scars is not going to win you a medal of compassion. The world has already decided the only reason for your scars is to educate those that do not have any as to how you inherited them. Meena our child bride has scars. Scars of humiliation combined with the blood-caked reminders of a life of submission; submission into a system that has taken away her dreams and replaced them with burden and toil. No, it is not right. Nevertheless, it exists. She is as real as the setting sun. In this day and age in the victimization of society, she is what the West calls a statistic of despondence. However, her despondence has respect. Her children will respect her and her authority. They will work to survive. They will also become statistics of despondence and the closest most of us will come to these kids will be on a "Feed the Children" commercial or a Discovery channel exclusive.

If we draw a parallel between a developing country like India or Thailand and compare it with living in the projects of Detroit or the "barrio" in Los Angeles, the irony would be breathtaking. Can you imagine the cry of the masses as they try to find the pedestal from where the launching of accusations can begin? Anthropology and sociology have explanations for our evolution into a reckless people. None of these explanations gives satisfaction to those that refuse to work.

In Dallas, Texas, it is not uncommon to find people who are hale and hearty sitting on a chair in their front lawn awaiting an eager government to send them fan mail rewarding their idleness.

Some are truly incapable of working and deserve the support of a government. However, will Meena and Mohan ever have that opportunity? Operating your day from the standpoint that you already have more than you deserve is what I am suggesting. It is my firm belief and unadulterated perspective that I have already received more than I deserve. If I do get more, I will be even more grateful for the opportunity to have tasted such lavish luxuries.

From Russia With Love

In July of 1997, I had the privilege of addressing a group of executives in Moscow on the concepts and ideas of Sales and Sales Management. To my amazement, their involvement in the session consisted of participation by a scant few. The irony is that of those who did participate, the ones who did it aggressively as instructed by me were Americans living in Russia. These people were earning their living in a country far away from mom and apple pie. I asked one of the gentlemen in the audience to identify the main differences in work ethic between the folks in America and those in Russia. His explanation is put in a bulleted form for easy understanding.

♣ Americans think that equality is a birthright. Russians think freedom is a struggle.

♣ Americans believe that everybody should be allowed to work. Russians believe that everybody should do the work.

♣ Americans expect to be treated fairly in the workplace.

Russians believe that disparity in the workplace will exist.

♣ Americans focus on the impenetrable ceiling and accuse it for their position. Russians believe that ceilings are meant to identify the demarcation necessary for social survival.

♣ Americans need time to themselves and demand vacations. Russians are afraid that time away from what they do will allow somebody else an opportunity to encroach into their space.

As free people in a free society our goal should be to continue to work hard and demand the very best from everyone else.

Follow Your Own Example

The stories told about the work ethic of Michael Jordan, Larry Bird, Jerry West and Jerry Rice, are legendary. These athletes excelled at their chosen trade and took their earning potential to new heights. If asked about the motivation behind their persistence, they would all point to someone in their family who was an influence.

What about the work ethic of an unwed mother? How about the demands of responsibility from a delinquent father? Consider the moral erosion of our neighborhoods and you will be greeted by the stench of laziness as it permeates the air of hopelessness. Taking pride in being able to work should come before anything. If the money you receive does not afford you the dignity you think you deserve, satisfy your wants with the dignity you can afford. Living within your means should not be that hard. Dignity comes from living a life on the money you earn.

Set a standard for your own achievement. Follow your own example. Create your own success category. Do not wait for the world to give you what you believe is your rightful share. There is no equality in the race of life. From the moment you are born to the moment you die, you will always compete for more than you need and more than you have. Fly to the ravaged towns of Rwanda where genocide has left an entire civilization without male children over the age of five. Ask them if they would trade places with you. Give them the option of coming out of their huts from midday temperatures that hover at 120° Fahrenheit, and tell them to flip burgers for minimum wage. Observe them for a week as they start to get comfortable and decide to invest in some learning at the community college. Follow them as they try to work hard and get another job. Before long they will be laughing and singing and sending money home to loved ones. As you observe this naked display of human emotion in progress, you will notice that they love the America the so-called poor of this country doubt. I honestly and sincerely believe that work is a privilege.

Boundaries of Effectiveness

In the days of the pioneers the common method used to acquire more than you had was to draw a boundary around the land and claim it for your own. Obviously, this ruffled the feathers of others who wanted the same land. In the Bible God asked Abraham to look as far as he could see and to look in all directions. The looking in all directions forced Abraham to have some boundaries. In our work, the avenues are unlimited and our potential, like

Abraham's, is as far as the eye can see. However, human beings in their wisdom decided to draw boundaries of ineffectiveness based on their own ability. The best way to chart a map of progress is to make the world your stage. Do not let anybody dictate to you the scope of your ability. If boundaries were followed throughout history the empires of old would not have flourished. Alexander would not have been great and England would not have succeeded in centuries of imperialist expansion. America would not have been discovered and we would not be having this conversation.

Man has always crossed boundaries to taste the fruits of forbidden lands. Tradition and temptation have yielded much of the world we live in. Succumbing to immoral temptation is the transgression that humanity has chosen. The greed to work more and earn more and the desire to get high on reward and recognition are the boundaries we must test in order to assure survival.

What are some of your perceived and impassable boundaries? What steps are you going to take to conquer those boundaries so you can have a renewed attempt at effectiveness?

_____

_____

_____

The World is Enough

Ian Fleming's mysterious man of intrigue who went by the digits 007 has captured our imagination as a globe-trotting, crime stopping one-man wrecking crew. Depicted on the big screen by a variety of men the persona of the man known as, James Bond, has left us all enamored. Chasing a thug on a moped in India could easily end up in a high-speed pursuit on the canals of Venice atop a speedboat laden with dynamite just for excitement. For this emissary of Her Majesty's Secret Service, the world was not enough to portray the exploits of one man's fantasy. Sitting in the new annex to London's Heathrow Airport I am reminded about how the world "is" enough in its existing grandeur and unlimited beauty. Looking through the panels of a business class lounge at the greenery in the distance I am amazed how finite all of this actually is. I left India for my first exploit with nine dollars in my pocket and a bucket full of fear, as I knew that my arrival in a new world would forever alter me.

The flight to Bucharest, Romania, this evening will culminate with me setting foot in the fiftieth country on my itinerant travelogue. Every continent has been visited except the frigid frontier where the only seminar attendees would be in tuxedos while marching single file to become a film. Truly the world is enough if little old me has seen so much in less than half my life. From the glaciers of Iceland, to the mesmerizing colors of the coral of the Great Barrier Reef, these simple eyes have said "enough." Gazing in wonder at the romance of Paris, and strolling down the capitalistic extravagance of Zurich, the eyes that were filled with fear have been stricken with awe. Projecting my voice in a coliseum in Greece to add mastery to my oratorical resume, and riding horseback on the Giza plateau while glibly wondering if the pharaohs intended me to do so, I have wept at my own fortune.

All it took was a piece of paper in a seminar in Dallas and a legendary motivator at the apex of his career inspiring me to want the entire world. His reminder, like the pages of a suspenseful novel, narrated the simplicity of hope and the uniqueness of a personal and passionate desire to see more, give more, and leave more. His gratitude remains reflected on the walls of the office that bear the scars of his sacrifice and the goodness of his name. My hero Zig Ziglar took a young immigrant boy with nine dollars in his pocket and a bucket of fear and turned him into a globe-trotting admirer of God's atlas. The world is enough if you want it to be enough for you. Your dreams are possible if you become disciplined enough to walk alongside them. The only high-speed chase worth its adrenaline is when you run to your destiny with purpose, knowing the God who created it all made it enough for all you need from it.

How much of this world do you really want? Are you willing to communicate with yourself on a sheet of paper and write down the possibilities that exist for you? Can you articulate in the space below what you think you should be proud of so you can begin to chart your desired course in the fulfillment of your dreams?

_____

_____

_____

The Axe of Tradition

It is graduation day in a small town and the proud father gives his son a gift. The son looks at the axe and solicits an explanation from his father. "This axe has been passed down in our family for many generations. My grandfather presented my father this axe. This axe is the very axe used by my great-grandfather to clear the land that has become our homestead." The son asks his father if it was the same axe or if they had made any changes. "We have replaced the handle a couple of times and replaced the head a couple of times. Other than that it is the same axe." This amusing story gives us great insight into tradition. The workplace has changed many handles and many heads, but the tradition of work is still the same. An honest day's work for an honest day's pay!

If you follow the steps in this book and answer the questions posed along the way, you will have begun a unique process of self-awareness and discovery. By investing in your potential as a creature that was wonderfully and fearfully made, you will begin to realize the treasures of the Creator. Imagine that you are already where many want to be. That means in the journey called life you are awake and have already begun to achieve the promise of effectiveness. When you begin to taste the glimpses of elusive hope, you will realize that a long time ago, before you were even conceived, God voted for you.

As I reflect on my personal good fortune to have shared my experiences with you, I would like to thank you, the reader, for your commitment to embracing the concepts and ideas. On a private note I would ask that you pray for this world that is in need of a reminder of the fragility of life and the innocence of relationships across cultural, religious and ethnic boundaries. I will close this book as I close all my offerings by simply saying:

I have traveled the world and the seven seas,

I have been on my highs and on my knees

But of all the good things that I have been privileged to do,

I thank God for dreams and I thank him for you.

I am Anila's husband and Nicolas' father saying thank you for reading. God Bless America and God Bless You.

CPSIA information can be obtained at www.ICGtesting.com
Printed in the USA
LVOW050304210513

334709LV00002B/4/P